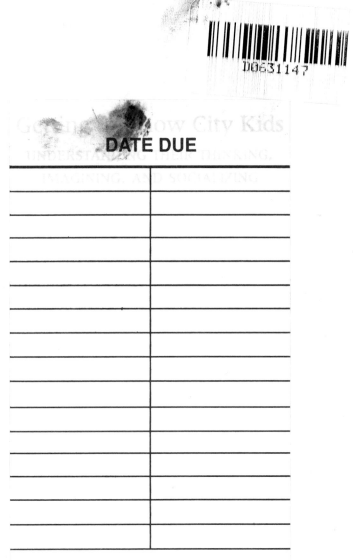

DATE DUE

Getting to Know City Kids

UNDERSTANDING THEIR THINKING, IMAGINING, AND SOCIALIZING

Sally Middlebrooks

FOREWORD BY

Eleanor Duckworth

Teachers College, Columbia University
New York and London

To my mother and sister
and to the memory of my father

Published by Teachers College Press, 1234 Amsterdam Avenue, New York, NY 10027

Library of Congress Cataloging-in-Publication Data

Middlebrooks, Sally.
    Getting to know city kids : understanding their thinking,
  imagining, and socializing / Sally Middlebrooks ; foreword by
  Eleanor Duckworth.
       p.   cm.
    Includes bibliographical references and index.
    ISBN 0-8077-3686-4 (cloth : alk. paper). — ISBN 0-8077-3685-6
  (pbk. : alk. paper)
    1. City children—United States.   2. City children—United States—
  Case studies.   3. Play—United States.   4. Child development—
  United States.   I. Title.
  HT206.M53   1998
  305.23'0973'091724—dc21   97-40580

ISBN 0-8077-3685-6 (paper)
ISBN 0-8077-3686-4 (cloth)

Printed on acid-free paper
Manufactured in the United States of America

05 04 03 02 01 00 99 98   8 7 6 5 4 3 2 1

Contents

Foreword

"By missing the 'secret places' where no one but children go, researchers have missed a significant part of children's lives," writes Sally Middlebrooks. Her book proceeds to take us to some of those secret places, and to show us how we might get to others without her. It also makes us want to.

The author has done a remarkable piece of work, entering into the play of six children from East Harlem, and asking them what it means to them. Early in the book she gives us a transcript of her conversation with Monifa Wright (the teacher who introduced her to the school community) in which she tries to anticipate the effects of her being an outsider to the children's worlds. "You blend in, you know," says Monifa. "Your mannerisms are easy for you to blend right in." It does not take many pages for us to see this happen. Middlebrooks is moved by profound respect in her wish to know about children's lives. And, as a long-time teacher in Boys' Clubs, children's museums, and Central Park Conservancy's "Castle" program, she knows how to make a genuine connection with the children. Her conversations with them are gems. It becomes clear that the fact that she is an outsider is beside the point.

She sees herself as a guest in the community. As a researcher, she does not limit herself to observing from a distance, drawing up questionnaires, marking check-lists. She goes wherever children will take her, and listens to all that they have to say. She is open to learn whatever there is to be learned, and her antennae pick up every fruitful lead.

And what is the interest of this work? "Why should adults know about children's play?" as she puts it to 10-year-old Rex. "So they could know them better," he replies. "If they want to have a conversation, they could have a better conversation with their child." This is, of course, important not only for parents but for teachers. The more teachers know about the activities and interests of their students, the more points of entry they have for connecting with their learning and taking it further.

There is another importance, too. This study is, in its specifics, about what urban children do and think as they build and play. But in these specifics, there is a powerful underlying message. Patricia Carini has a wonderful story about a longitudinal study of seven school children that she carried out over seven years. When she presented the study to members of the school system, describing and discussing each of the children in great detail, one response was, "Isn't it lucky that you happened upon seven such interesting children!" The point is, of course, that all children are interesting if we accept the job of getting to know them. And in this book Sally Middlebrooks shows us convincingly that urban children are not only interesting, but resilient, capable, imaginative, smart.

Middlebrooks takes us into the private worlds of six children. As educators, we are in her debt for opening those worlds to us, for adding dimensions to our understanding of the lives of the children we teach, for expanding our ways of connecting with them.

Eleanor Duckworth
Harvard Graduate School of Education

Preface

The one photo I possess of myself as a child shows me sitting in a wooden wheelbarrow with three playmates. I look to be about 5 years old. My father, the builder of the wheelbarrow, is standing behind us, hands on hips and looking strong, even though the dark hair he married my mother with has receded to the edges of his head. The other girl in the photo, the neighborhood's aspiring ballerina, wears a large ribbon in her hair; I wear a paper pirate's hat, black with white skull and crossbones. We are in the driveway next to the house in Jacksonville, Florida, where I grew up.

Beginning when I was 6 years old, I walked each morning down this same driveway (later, I rode my bike), almost in a straight line, for two blocks to a one-story, red-brick school building. I don't remember school as vividly as I remember the days and evenings or the long afternoons after school or the hot summers in between grades. It was then that the driveway became my stage for going places: for example, a river on which a wooden wagon could be converted into a boat simply by adding a triangular-shaped piece of wood to its front to make a deck.

Our driveway led into a garage. In the photo, the door is open, making the darkened interior appear cavelike. It was here that my father made things and where he stored his tools. There were nails in numerous bottles and a large box holding wood of different kinds and shapes. There was a long work counter, a tablesaw I was forbidden to touch, a hammer that was mine. It was here that I watched my father make a 16-foot speedboat and carefully paint its mahogany deck. It was here I made plans and tried to make things myself.

The photo also shows the kitchen door of my house and, beside it, a line of shrubbery. A variety of plants circumscribed the house. Some, like the azaleas, bloomed in early spring; others, like the tall poinsettias, opened into red stars that thrilled us with the nearness of Christmas. Our yard was small—no jungle or rain forest—but there was diversity and luxurious-ness and surprise. The kumquat tree in the front yard, with its low limbs, was just right for climbing and for perching in unseen; the live oak next to the driveway towered above all houses on the street and marked the entrance to our driveway. "Turn here," it said to me, "this is home."

Within this small world I played and played out my growing up. Of course, there were anger, tears, jealousies, and I recall once making sling-shots and collecting ammo for a war waged behind garbage cans, but I do not recall the actual fighting. A world war had recently ended, and on the home front we children were made safe by the times and by adults who, though not often visible, were nearby.

As I look again at the photograph, I see that what was compelling for me as a child continues meaningful and persistent for me as a teacher and researcher: a curiosity about the natural world, a passion for making things and for transforming spaces, and a sense of delight in being among children.

Acknowledgments

I am grateful to many people for their contributions to the making of this book.

First, I want to thank the children whose stories I try to tell here. I feel privileged by their trust in me. In the same breath, I acknowledge my gratitude to the teacher, who wishes to be called Monifa Wright in the narrative. She was my "bridge" to the children, their parents, and teachers. Friend, colleague, and mentor, I continue to learn from our conversations.

There are too many among the Harvard Graduate School of Education community whose regard and care sustained me during the making of this book to name them all, but I must recognize several. As advisor to my doctoral work, Claryce Evans combined deep insight with broad humor, successfully guiding me through the ups and downs of being a student again. I am also grateful to three groups associated with the Graduate School: the staff at the *Harvard Educational Review*, who were never too busy to make me feel at home; my Teaching, Curriculum, and Learning Environments cohort, who became my extended family, fiercely loyal and supportive; and Annie Rogers and the women with whom I played baseball or—my name for these Saturday gatherings—"relational hardball."

To those who read parts of this work as it progressed and the many others who talked with me about it, I am deeply appreciative. I would like this book to be worthy of their respect. They include Eleanor Duckworth, Sheldon White, Heidi Watts, Brenda Engel, Karen Maloney, Florence Ladd, and Mary Rogers. And I wish to express my special thanks to four mothers—Gladys Capella Noya, Ellen Doris, Evangeline Stefanakis, and Denise Zinn—whose arms embrace hope and change.

Finally, I thank Irwin Block, who told me seven years ago, "Sally, stop talking—go do it." I have.

PART I

Context

1 "One of Them Kids"

We make it real 'cause we act like we really, we really are a mother and that we really own our own house.

With these words, fifth-grader Michelle describes the world of home and community she builds with her girlfriends in the small playground of the housing project where they live in an inner-city neighborhood. The world the girls imagine reflects life both as they know it and as they would like it to be. Michelle continues:

I pretend that we play house and we got a big house and we have money to go buy cars and stuff. And my friend, her cousins be our children. And then we pretend to go shopping. Then, when we find coupons, we pretend that's money and then we go spend it. And that's it.

Michelle takes her play seriously; she explains its purposes as follows:

So when we play this, we want to see how it feels to be a mother or a person that works on the job. So when we grow up, we'll know things about being a mother and being a person that works at a bank or being a person who has to run around and find a baby-sitter.

SIX WORLDMAKERS

Michelle[1] is one of the six children whose play I present in this book. Specifically, I describe one feature of the children's play, what I call *world-*

---

1. Michelle and the other five children participating in this study gave themselves pseudonyms. I chose the names for the other children.

making. By worldmaking, I mean the three-dimensional structures children build and then inhabit. Unlike play supervised by adults, worldmaking is constructed for and by kids, away from adult eyes. It is self-chosen and self-initiated. As settlers, homeowners, and club members, children lay claim to real estate. While some children in rural settings are outdoors digging a network of caves in a river bank or building forts in a wood, some of their city cousins have dragged a cardboard box and a rug to the edge of a playground, bought soda and chips, and settled in until supper. At the edges of the world, in places adults relinquish—closets, bedrooms, playgrounds, vacant lots—children build and play.

Like a lab or workshop, these are spaces where children actively construct worlds from materials at hand; where, having reduced the world to a smaller, more manageable size, "they sort out the nature of reality and explore possibilities and impossibilities in their situation" (Phyllis Hostler, 1959, quoted in Newson & Newson, 1979, p. 103). These worlds become children's private universes—the arena for hatching plots, the shelter to return to when wounded, the stage on which to try out various adult-related tasks, roles, and relationships, including membership in family and community.

The three girls and three boys whom I introduce below are African American and Puerto Rican. They live in apartments—either in a housing project, a tenement, or a recently renovated building in East Harlem, a densely populated New York City neighborhood plagued by poverty, crime, drugs, and high infant mortality (see Appendix A). The children range in age from 8 to 12 years and attend the same public school. During the period 1993–1995, two of the six children lived with both parents, two with their mothers, and two with grandmothers. A year later, family and financial circumstances having shifted, three children moved out of the neighborhood, one to reunite with her mother.

Brenda. Born in May 1985, Brenda is the youngest of the six children whose stories I tell here. She lives with her mother and a foster child whom she calls "baby brother." Brenda is of Puerto Rican background but is monolingual, speaking English at home and at school. The family lives in a housing development residents refer to as "the projects." The seven-story building where Brenda lives is just across from the school where she is a third grader. On weekends and most afternoons, Brenda plays inside her apartment with Catherine, her younger female cousin. In the late spring, they were joined in their play by Mandy, Brenda's new "best friend," a girl her own age. The girls transform spaces and objects in Brenda's bedroom into a stage for "playing house" and "camping out" (bedroom's measurements according to Brenda: 108" by 130"). Next to her bed, Brenda puts up a "teepee" by placing her pink satin bedcover over two chairs. The photos that Brenda took with the disposable camera I gave her show not only the teepee, its location, and how it is built; they also show that her room is full of things—her things. In addition to the bed and teepee, there is a TV, dolls and stuffed animals crowd the shelves, and a large poster of a dog hangs on the wall.

Isaac. Born in June 1985, Isaac lives with his mother, father, and one older brother in a recently built apartment building facing a busy avenue (the oldest brother is away at school). Isaac's mother works as a paraprofessional in the school where he is a third grader, and after becoming involved with this project by taking photographs of her son at play, she spoke at length with me about what she had learned. Like Brenda's, Isaac's family is of Puerto Rican background; but unlike Brenda, Isaac speaks some Spanish. He pointed out to me twice during our three conversations when he was speaking Spanish (he used the words *cocha* and *la sala*). When I asked if he talked in Spanish when playing, he replied negatively. Allowed outdoors only when accompanied by a parent, Isaac plays mostly indoors. As shown in the photographs, the bedroom Isaac shares with his brother is neat and orderly (measurements, carried out by Isaac, came to 9'6" by 13'11"). There he enjoys playing video games with boys his age who live in the same building, and he sometimes wrestles with his older brother. But, more often, Isaac plays alone with his set of GI Joes, devising battles and sneak attacks. He sometimes makes what he refers to as "a little house" using two blankets to cover both sides of the lower part of the bunk beds he shares with his brother. Shielded by the blankets, he lies on his bed, reading, making "funny noises," and playing with his favorite stuffed animals.

Michael. Born in April 1983, Michael lives with his mother, father, and younger brother, Allen, in a five-story apartment building that faces a busy avenue. Although a city park is just across the street, Michael is not allowed to go there on his own. He is looking forward to playing basketball as part of an after-school program that is promised to begin sometime soon. The family is also of Puerto Rican background; Michael speaks English at school and at home. He is in the fifth grade and is described by teachers as "the class clown." Michael enlivened our conversations, and his fast-paced and good-humored narration allowed me to see the dramas he plays out at home, frame by frame. When one or both parents are home, the boys' play is confined to their bedroom, a small, ordered space, which Michael says measures 12' by 13'. On the floor of the bedroom, in front of the boys' bunk beds, Michael carefully positions three to four pillows and a blanket to build two specific structures. One is for playing cops and robbers; the other for the play the brothers call "casino."

Michelle. Born in August 1983, Michelle is African American. A student in a fourth-fifth grade combination, she was chosen in June to be a member of the color guard, which was to precede the sixth graders at their graduation. Michelle lives with her grandmother and two male cousins in "the projects"; she is in contact with her mother, who lives across town. Her best friend is Ayisha, also a fifth grader and the child I describe next. With other girls, all older than they, Michelle and Ayisha turn the outdoor space between their two buildings into a world in which they are mothers and sisters, own their own home (the large, metal climbing tower), go shopping, go to parties, and take care of their "children." Sometimes they set up a store, "buying" items with coupons or pretending they have money. Michelle's cousin, Emet, the same age, often participates in the girls' play. Outdoors, he may be a monster who chases them or the baby-sitter who minds their "children"; indoors, he takes the part of the bank depositor in the bank where the girls are tellers. The previous summer, Ayisha and Michelle, with the help of another boy, Gerard, who had nails and improvised a hammer, built a clubhouse in a crabapple tree, located on a busy corner of the housing development where they all live.

Ayisha. Born in September 1983, Ayisha is of Puerto Rican background. She lives in the building across from Michelle with her grandparents, one aunt, and two uncles. As best friends, Ayisha and Michelle play house inside Michelle's apartment and outside in the playground. In warm weather, when not playing house, the girls go to the public pool located in a nearby park. They also skate on the sidewalks that crisscross the development, and, when it's raining, they seek the shelter of an entrance way to play a commercial board game called Girl Talk. Ayisha spoke of plans to form a "Baby-Sitters' Club" over the summer; the officers were already in place (she is vice-president). As for the clubhouse in the crab-apple tree, Ayisha could see it from her window. She dreams that a rope ladder connects that high place both with her apartment and with the stores across the street.

Rex. Born in October 1983, Rex is in the fifth grade. Like Michelle, he is African American. He lives with his mother and older brother in a newly renovated building on a side street. The lack of traffic allows for an active outdoor life, with Rex joining boys his age and older for football games in the street, where manhole covers represent goal lines. Games of hide-and-seek in a backyard have been curtailed because of a neighbor's complaints.

Although he and Michael are pals at school, the boys do not play together after school. Rex played actively indoors when he was younger. He recalls playing games of hide-and-seek and pretending to be a Ninja Turtle when friends came over. Older now, he's often on his own at home. The drama is an interior one. In his living room, he puts a sheet or coverlet over two chairs and sits quietly and snugly underneath. He refers to this place as "like an Eskimo thing." It's warm there, and he says that inside he feels "isolated from the rest of the world."

A hundred years ago, the philosopher William James (1890/1983) described what he saw as a universal "instinct" for "constructiveness" in human beings—as well as in bees and beavers. He wrote that even at an early age, we remodel "things that are plastic . . . into shapes that are [their] own." He goes on: "And the remodeling, however useless it may be, gives . . . more pleasure than the original thing" (p. 1043). "Habitation," according to James, is a prominent form of constructiveness. It is our "instinct to seek a sheltered nook" into which we may "retire and be safe" (pp. 1044–1045). James provides these two examples:

> We feign a shelter within a shelter, by backing up beds in rooms . . . We see children today, when playing in wild places, take the greatest delight in discovering and appropriating such retreats and "playing house" there. (pp. 425–426)

Underlying James's statement is the belief that children are predisposed to pretend shelters inside bedrooms and to build retreats in the "wild places" of their environment. But what about children who live in small, crowded city apartments and whose "wild places" are in the urban environment—in other words, poor city kids?

RESEARCH ON CHILDREN'S PLAY

Research on children's play ultimately involves a discussion of the nature and function of childhood itself. It is not surprising, then, that during the past century, interest in what children prefer to play, at what age, with whom, and where has attracted researchers from diverse fields, including psychology, folklore, anthropology, sociology, history, architecture, and urban design.

Two studies at the turn of the century illustrate the widespread interest in children across disciplines that has continued for the past hundred years. Writing in the fourth volume of *Journal of American Folk-lore*, Culin (1891) describes outdoor games boys play in Brooklyn, New York, as described to him by "a lad of ten years" (p. 221). Games are modified, he concludes, to suit city life; for example, iron lamp-posts replace trees in games of tag. Basing his findings on responses to a questionnaire mailed to select teachers across the United States, Acher (1904), a colleague of G. Stanley Hall, divides children's outdoor play according to the materials used—sand, stones, and snow—and by gender and age. Acher also offers some advice. His message is both revelatory and cautionary, and although he may have meant his advice for teachers, researchers might listen as well. He writes:

> The one thing which such a study as this reveals is that children have their own point of view, many times radically different from that of the adult. One must first try to understand children and get their point of view if one is to treat them sympathetically and be helpful to them. (p. 143)

Despite the relatively long and persistent interest in children and youth in the United States over the past hundred years, the research landscape remains thinly settled, with ages and stages ignored and children's play spaces unobserved. Moreover, thinly veiled in much of this research are two beliefs: that what children do and play when they are on their own is not worthwhile and that cities are bleak and brutal—"unnatural" places for children to grow up in. The beliefs merge in the research on city kids. Methods researchers have used—and not used—also contribute to what amounts to a slight and superficial exploration of the everyday lives of children in general and those of city kids in particular. Whereas few studies contradict the deficit model, material culture presents a radically different view.

Gaps

Library shelves show the unevenness of the research effort. First, while children's play during early childhood is well documented in the litera-ture, this is not the case for children in middle childhood, especially con-cerning what they do on their own (Rogoff, 1990; Wright, 1960). Second, the study of children during the past century has been largely confined to the laboratory and the classroom (White & Siegel, 1984; Wright, 1960), with research outside these experimental environments focused primarily on what children do and play in other kinds of adult-supervised settings, such as schoolyards and playgrounds (see, among others, Finnan, 1988; Glassner, 1976; Lever, 1976; Sluckin, 1981; Sutton-Smith, 1982), and as members of organized groups led by adults (see Mechling, 1980, for ex-ample, for a discussion of the Boy Scouts). Consequently, little is known about children's lives outside of school when they are on their own—

specifically, both "how children transform the real space of the environment into the imagined space or setting of play" (Franklin, 1983, p. 211) and what "qualities" different environments provide for children's play (Hart, 1979, p. 165). Third, even those researchers who have studied children's unsupervised play have ignored what children play and do *inside* their homes. Fourth, although the everyday lives of children living in small towns in the United States are richly documented (see Barker & Wright, 1951/1966; Hart, 1979), the everyday lives of city children are less documented.

Deficit Model

Although sparse, the information about the everyday lives of city kids is nevertheless presented as authoritative (see Brace, 1872; Covello, 1958/ 1970; Hawes & Hiner, 1985). For example, surveying city streets at the turn of the century, psychologist and early playground reformer Henry Stoddard Curtis observed: "No one who has observed children carefully in any city . . . between the close of school and supper, has found that any considerable percentage of them were doing anything that was worthwhile" (Curtis, about 1915, quoted in Boyer, 1978, p. 244).

Sixty years later, observing urban children and youth in public housing projects, sociologist Franklin D. Becker (1976) reports: "What seems so bleak about the [children's] play was not the location per se, but that most of the children observed were engaged in completely passive activities: sitting and standing and watching others or just talking" (p. 564). Summing up, Becker writes that city children are unable to act as "effective change agents—capable of controlling as well as being controlled" (p. 545).

"Location per se," however, is given prominence in much of the literature, and poor urban neighborhoods are presented as having few qualities that support and promote children's play. The two examples that follow typify this point of view. Architect and playground designer Robin Moore (1980), basing his conclusions on children's maps of their neighborhoods, one drawn by a girl from downtown Oakland and the other by a girl living not far away, but in the country, claims that the inner-city child lacks almost "any kind of imageable relationship with her environment" (p. 128) and, as a result, will grow up "incompetent" (p. 128). And noted urban designer Clare Cooper (1970), contrasting her observations of children at play outdoors in cities with those in the country, writes: "The city-child, deprived of the opportunities afforded the country-child to play in woods, trees . . . is deprived in a much deeper, psychological sense of the ability to learn through experimenting" (p. 21).

Whether at the turn of the century or more recently, reformers and researchers idealize the "natural" environment and demonize the urban environment. The message consistently conveyed is that an ugly and harsh physical environment prevails in the city. Partially as a result, the majority of research has centered on interpreting the consequences for children's development resulting from the "unnaturalness" or "bleakness" of the urban environment (Becker, 1976; Brace, 1872; Cooper Marcus & Moore, 1976; Hall, 1907/1975; Michelson, Levine, & Spina, 1979; W. Moore, 1969; Riis, 1890/1971; Wohlwill & Heft, 1987). It has followed that city children—economically poor children, in particular—are portrayed not only as disadvantaged but also as deficient (Howard & Scott, 1981). Researchers' beliefs about city kids guide their questions, shape their observations, and are sieves through which data are sifted.

Different Views

Given the prevailing belief in a deficit model that underlies empirical research, it is not surprising that I have found only two studies that describe the resiliency and creativity of children living in urban environments. Moreover, the deficit model is refuted by many outside the research domain—photographers, for example, as I will explain.

Two Studies. Psychologists Berg and Medrich (1980) marvel at the resilience of kids who lay claim to a "secret spot" near a stream "cluttered with broken glass and dead wood" (p. 336). In contrast, Zerner (1977), an urban designer, sees the availability of waste spaces and broken, discarded materials as resources for children's play. Children, he believes, are drawn to these "fantastic places, half metallic ruin and half riot of the vegetable kingdom" (p. 28). Even a "weedy lot" (p. 28) is a valued preserve "in which the cultural and natural worlds mingle in a wealth of disarray" (p. 30).

Zerner includes only six lines spoken by three children, while Berg and Medrich include none. These studies, though illuminating about the everyday lives of city kids, are incomplete. Still missing are children's perspectives of the built worlds they create and inhabit. The hunt for other, more satisfactory approaches continues with an exploration next of what material culture, using the lenses of camera and memory, tells us about city kids and their play.

Material Culture. Material culture presents a portrait of children's everyday lives in cities similar to that reported by Zerner and by Berg and Medrich. Singly and in combination, photographs and documentary films, fiction, personal commentary, and memory provide a rich, substantial, and authentic portrait of the lives of children in cities, one that puts into question the large body of research detailed earlier.

Photographs by Helen Levitt (1987, 1989) and Martha Cooper (1990), for example, and the documentary film *My Own Yard to Play In* by Lerner (1959), show children at play on streets and sidewalks and in vacant lots in New York City from the 1940s to the 1980s. Levitt's photographs also remind us of how children, although largely confined to the margins and edges of the adult world and limited in their resources, make things happen and have fun. In one of my favorite Levitt photographs (1989, p. 16), a group of boys of mixed ages float pieces of a broken mirror in a curbside "stream"; in another, children play in the "river" created by an open hydrant (1989, p. 15).

Another example from outside the research literature that contributes to a fuller picture of what city kids do and play is author Tillie Olsen's (1974) fictional account of growing up poor in the United States in the 1920s. In her description of children's imaginative play at the city dump, she calls into question other literatures that present only poor children's alleged deficiencies. Olsen writes:

> Children—already stratified as dummies in school, condemned as unfit for the worlds of learning art, imagination, invention—plan, measure, figure, design, invent, construct, costume themselves, stage dramas. . . . On the inexhaustible dump strange structures rise: lookout towers, sets, ships, tents, forts, lean-tos, clubhouses, cities and stores . . . pretend palaces. (p. 121)

The observations of urban historian Jane Jacobs (1961) also capture the variety, spontaneity, and flexibility of children's play on city streets—in this case, the streets of New York's West Village in the 1950s. That children would have to adapt to "urban renewal" angered Jacobs. She took the position that much that was good about urban life would be lost to the bulldozer as blocks of tenements were replaced with housing projects (for example, in another part of the city, the projects where three children in this study, Brenda, Michelle, and Ayisha, live). Although I do not attempt here to compare and contrast the quality of life for children before and after the housing projects, Jacobs's description is valuable because it shows how children go about using what time they have as well as the things and spaces of their environment for their play. She writes:

> A great part of children's outdoor play . . . occurs at incidental times and must be sandwiched in. A lot of outdoor life for children adds up from bits. . . . It happens after school while children may be pondering what to do and wondering who will turn up. . . . They slop in puddles, write with chalk, jump rope, roller skate, shoot marbles, trot out their possessions, converse, trade

cards, play stoop ball, walk stilts, decorate soap-box scooters, dismember baby
carriages, climb on railings, run up and down. (pp. 85–86)

Consider, for example, a short, but informative report that follows about
growing up in East Harlem at the turn of the century. The author is Leonard
Covello, who is remembered as the first Italian principal of East Harlem's
Benjamin Franklin High School (1934–1957). In his autobiography, *The
Heart Is the Teacher*, Covello (1958/1970) takes us to places only he knew.
He reports that as a boy he fought, stole, played cops and robbers, and was
a treasure hunter. He calls his secret place a "hideout."

We fought the Second Avenue gang with rocks and tin cans and used garbage-
can covers for shields. We scavenged the dumps and the river front for anything we could sell to make a penny. We had a hideout under the tenement
rubble where we played cops and robbers and took the fruit and sweet pota-
toes stolen from the pushcarts to cook in our "mickey-cans." (p. 34)

The Need for Different Approaches

There are no pushcarts now in East Harlem, and other things have changed
as well. Do children continue to hide out, play cops and robbers, cook on
improvised stoves? To find children at play, we need research approaches
that are particular to children and to what they play (Bauman, 1982; Fine
& Sandstrom, 1988; Garbarino & Stott, 1989).

The English folklorists Iona and Peter Opie (1969/1984) add this consideration—where children play. They conclude that the places children
"like best are the secret places 'where no one goes'" (p. 15). Similarly, others
suggest that when children play in the less crowded and more private
spaces outdoors, they may play less stereotypically—in mixed groups, for
example (Becker, 1976; Berg & Medrich, 1980; Thorne, 1993; Zerner,
1977). By ignoring or not seeking out the "secret places" where only children go, researchers have missed a significant part of children's lives. But
how do we gain entry?

In his book *Children's Experience of Place*, geographer Roger Hart (1979)
shares in some detail how he came to learn about children's outdoor play
in a small town in rural Vermont. I count seven methods in all. They are
children's diaries, time sampling, model-building, interviews with children,
interviews with parents, participant observation, and child-led walks. Two
examples from this list and Hart's evaluation of each follow.

Providing children with aerial photographs showing the town where
they live, Hart instructs them to identify those places they like and dis-
like, and those that are dangerous and frightening. He concludes that chil-

dren use a common stockpile of answers and do not express what is personally important to them. Following children's lead on walks, he concludes that they are more likely to share their hiding places, their secret paths, and the places where they like to be alone (he uses a Polaroid camera to record these special places as the children point them out). Hart writes, "The more I allowed myself to be 'led' by a child, the more I experienced that child's environment" (p. 184).

Hart pauses in his description of the shelters, playhouses, and forts these rural kids build to question the capacity of the urban environment to support children's play. He writes:

> Rural areas offer more opportunity for building due to the availability of both unused space and loose parts. It may be that cities also offer these qualities, but we must await the comparative in-depth study of children's use and experience of environments before we can say this with any certainty. (p. 165)

With this study I address Hart's call for an in-depth study of children's unsupervised play in the urban environment. The multitextured portraits of city kids presented here are, in large part, the result of my choosing multiple methods of data collection, each aimed at eliciting the child's point of view. Taken together, the drawings, the photographs, and the voices of the children help provide a richly detailed view of children's thinking, intentions, and purposes, revealing the private, hidden worlds of childhood in the urban environment.

SIGNS SAYING "UNDER CONSTRUCTION"

I look at the drawing by 9-year-old Stacey, a child I talked with in the first stages of this study, who told me she built a playhouse in a park where she goes after school and on weekends with another girl and three boys, all her age. Stacey's drawing shows a house with a door, four windows, peaked roof, and chimney (see Figure 1.1). What interests me is the smoke curling from the chimney. For me it's a sign that this place is occupied. People are inside. "It feels homey-like; the clubhouse feels like home," Stacey told me. "It's comfy . . . It's like your living room."

As I told the children participating in this project, "We're on a mission," I may have sounded as if I was caricaturing a TV detective or spy thriller, but I meant to—and I was not joking. Smoke, a cardboard box, wood nailed to a tree branch, a sheet over two chairs—all possible clues that we are on the trail that will lead us to the secret, private worlds of children.

Figure 1.1. Stacey's Playhouse

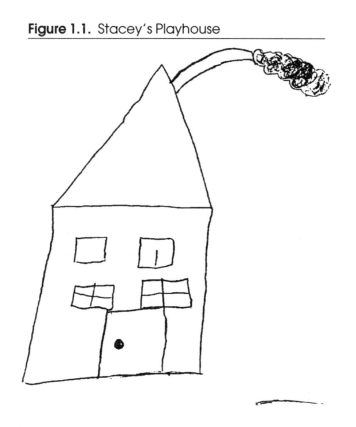

Some Findings

Like colorful threads in a weaving, three main themes emerge from this study only to be rewoven. Additionally, according to the child telling his or her story, the themes will vary—in their thickness and brightness, for example, as well as in the overall pattern they display.

"The Ability to Create the World." This study reveals children's world-making as a creative act. As child psychiatrist Donald Winnicott (1983) maintains, creativity is "the ability to create the world" (p. 40). And as 10-year-old Ayisha says of her drawing of the clubhouse she made with her best friend Michelle: "And this shows you what we was imaginating and what this would look like if we put our minds to it." What children "put their minds to," what they build and what they imagine, is the subject of this book.

No matter how cheap, fragile, and transitory, or however ignored or dismissed, the physical and social worlds children build and inhabit connect them to what the philosopher John Dewey (1934/1980) calls the "enduring values of collective human life" (p. 221). While Dewey is referring to the adult field of architecture, in the quotation that follows there is room for Ayisha's clubhouse. Dewey writes:

> Architecture "represents" the memories, hopes, fears, purposes, and sacred values of those who build in order to shelter a family, provide an altar for the gods, establish a place in which to make laws, or set up a stronghold against attack. . . . Every important structure is a treasury of storied memories and a monumental registering of cherished expectancies for the future. (pp. 221–222)

The Stuff of Stories. The environments children build for themselves offer platforms or stages for their stories. We "act like," the children say when describing what they *do* inside. Their stories come from what's familiar to them. Plots and characters are taken from what they've seen on television and in the movies, what they've done in school, what they've heard from others, and from their everyday experiences as members of a family and a community. In other words, as we will see in the stories that follow, children play what they've noticed in the world around them. A short list of what they've noticed includes:

- Relationships among family members
- Roles men and women play and don't play
- The work adults do
- Representations of power and authority
- Symbols of membership and belonging
- What's scary
- What's fair and unfair
- Exchanges and transactions between and among people

As for the material and props children need for their stories, if the real things are unavailable, children make them or find something comparable in form or function. And if they can do neither, they imagine them. The following examples help make clear what I mean by these three possible ways of working. When Michael plays cops and robbers with his younger brother, the paper money the robber steals is from the boys' Monopoly game; likewise, when Michelle plays house, she pays the "fake babysitter" with Monopoly money. Pretending she is camping out in her bedroom, Brenda cuts a brown paper bag, colors it red and yellow, and, over this "fire," pretends to roast marshmallows. When Ayisha plays house outdoors, friends bring down a wooden board. They use this piece of wood as the countertop for their grocery store where the "mothers" shop.

Bounded, yet Open to Possibility. In bedrooms or on playgrounds, under sheets or inside cardboard boxes, children "sort out the nature of reality and explore possibilities and impossibilities in their situation" (Newson & Newson, 1979, p. 103). "Worldmaking as we know it," writes the philosopher Nelson Goodman (1978), "always starts from worlds at hand; the making is the remaking" (p. 6).

By making some form of habitation, children provide themselves with a particular space—a place just for them. These spaces are bounded; they offer protection and shelter; within them, children can say:

Here I am/we are.
Here I/we do what I/we want to do.
Here I/we can be who I/we want to be.

And as we will see later on and in more detail, these environments allow children to do one or more of the following:

- To have fun
- To find refuge—to hide out; to retire to and be safe
- To be with and among friends; to explore and develop relationships
- To organize experience with flexibility, ingenuity, and daring
- To objectify experience: to play out different roles—what mothers, cops, and villains do, for example
- To experiment with authority and power
- To take some measure of control
- To turn ordinary materials into a three-dimensional structure that stands, stays up, and holds together
- To feel good, proud, and successful

This study shows poor city children neither as passive victims of their environment nor as monsters—products of "unnatural" surroundings—but, instead, as active, normal children who bravely imagine new worlds and try to build them.

Other Play, Other Questions, and Final Points

In this study I attempt to understand how some children make sense of themselves, others, and the world through the three-dimensional structures they build. I feel sure I could have begun elsewhere—with the handclapping games some girls play, for example, chase games, games of hide-and-seek, or planting flowers, and so on. By choosing to look closely at only one feature of children's play, it is not my intention to dismiss or diminish other play types, but rather to concentrate.

In addition to the need to explore other types of children's play, three larger questions remain for others to continue. They are:

- What helps researchers and teachers to learn about children?
- To what extent can we really understand children's sense of themselves and the world around them?
- What do particular children tell us about all children?

Finally, these two points. Although the interpretations I draw from my analysis of these six childrens' descriptions of their worldmaking activities may not be generalizable to other children, they are, however, consistent with what I have learned from other children I have interviewed and observed (e.g., 64 children interviewed in a pilot study conducted in 1990–1991). At the same time, I caution readers to avoid seeing the children who tell their stories here as "exceptional"; what I mean by this is seeing the children as "exceptions" to all those other children who live and play in the inner-city neighborhoods of this country. That perception does not push at the stereotypes we hold. Rather I hope that the children readers meet in these pages challenge simplistic, one-dimensional, and uncritical assessments about children in general and about children of color in particular.

I am reminded that the impetus for this book began when, curious about what city kids I knew did on their own, I decided to ask them. Fortunately, early on I met an 11-year-old boy named Sean. His words guided this work and continue to reverberate in my thoughts. Sean told me:

You have to understand, we're not like no angels or nothing. So we be doing some bad stuff, but not always. . . . Like me. If you saw me, you would think like that—like I was one of them kids. But if you talk to us, talk to us, then you'd really understand how smart we are.

FORMAT OF THIS BOOK

The remainder of this book principally divides into two parts. In the first, the discussion considers in some detail the approaches I used to enter into the 3-dimensional structures six children build and to try to understand the worlds they create within. Descriptions of what six children do and play then follow in Part II, making up the core of the book. Finally, concluding the book are some things I learned and possible implications for city teachers.

While it is obvious that this book focuses on but a small piece of the immense puzzle of human development and that more studies of what I attempted to investigate and what I left undone are needed, my intent is a provocative one. Guided by the children, I go behind the scenes to unveil something of the breadth and depth of their curiosity, industry, and imagination—features seldom called upon by schools. Knowledge of such resilience and creativity is a cause for hope and a call for change. Specifically, I hope this book will stimulate alternative approaches to looking at children's capacities to learn and grow and will urge teachers to build on and extend the complexity of children's play as it relates to the intellectual work—and play—of the classroom.

2 Mapping My Route

In this chapter I review where I've come from, starting with the questions I had about children's play and continuing with the uneven course of looking for children who specifically report building three-dimensional structures. I move from the neighborhood where the children live and play to their family arrangements and the interior spaces where they play and build. I report on the concerns and difficulties I encountered and how, slowly, through the help of someone close to the children, I began to feel and act less like an outsider and more like an insider.

MY QUESTIONS

How do children 8 to 11 or 12 years old, who live in economically disadvantaged urban neighborhoods, describe the three-dimensional worlds they construct for themselves and then inhabit? Within this question, I explored five main areas of inquiry, as follows:

1. What do children report about the three-dimensional structures they build? For example, what do they say about the crew, about materials, design, construction, and location of the structures they build? Additionally, what do they say about origins and purposes?
2. What do children report about the worlds *inside* their constructions? For example, what do they say about their co-settlers, about rules and rituals, about who's "in" and who's "out" and why?
3. How do children describe their feelings about playing on their own? For example, what do they say about the role of adults in their "unsupervised" play? What do they say about feeling safe?
4. What do boys report, and what do girls? How are these reports the same, and how are they different?

5. What is important for educators, parents, and other caregivers to understand and know? And do the children themselves have something to say about that?

Looking for Worldmakers

To find third through sixth graders who build three-dimensional structures as part of their indoor or outdoor play, I looked for a majority/minority elementary school in a so-called inner-city neighborhood. The following were my criteria:

1. A "neighborhood" school, meaning that the majority of children come from the surrounding area and walk to school (as I will explain later, the physical environment is more complex than I assumed—each block, each street is often very different from another)
2. A school that reflects the so-called minority populations who make up the majority of people who live in the poorest urban neighborhoods in the Northeast (two-thirds of the students at the site selected are African American and one third are Latino), but one that is not bilingual—I am monolingual
3. A "typical" school; that is, a school with no special focus (e.g., science or art)
4. A school where the majority of students are eligible for free breakfast and lunch programs (95% at the site selected)

Finding a "Bridge"

I believed children would more readily accept my questions and teachers would be more willing to tolerate my presence and requests if school personnel already knew me. As manager of Belvedere Castle for the Central Park Conservancy, I knew teachers and principals in many Manhattan elementary schools. Although I had been away from New York for 3 years, it took only three telephone calls before I found a teacher who agreed to work with me. The teacher was Monifa Wright (pseudonym).

Monifa, like me, is in her fifties. She is biracial and grew up in Harlem, where she now lives; I am European-American and grew up in the South. She has two children in their twenties; I have no children. Monifa has taught in the same school in East Harlem for 22 years; I have worked in informal educational settings with city kids for 15 years (the castle in Central Park, a boys' club in East Harlem, an after-school program in Hell's Kitchen). Monifa and I met in the mid-1980s when she attended workshops I led for New York City teachers who wanted to take their classes on field trips to Central Park. Later, when a teachers' advisory board for Park programs was formed, my colleagues and I invited Monifa to be among its members.

When Monifa was unexpectedly absent for my first visit to the school in March 1994, I nevertheless went ahead as planned and interviewed children from two third-grade classrooms. (Monifa had given out permission forms to students in each class, and 10 or so forms had already been returned.) The interviews went fine, the teachers were helpful, but, as I wrote in my journal, "starting out" was full of uncertainties:

> This feels lonely. Just me. Although I'm dependent on so many others, I feel as if I am crossing/invading cultures and terrain; that in this school, with its myriad relationships and feuds, I am treading on toes, walking across turfs with little knowledge—sensing that a minefield is located just beneath my feet.

Thus I realized early on that Monifa's presence, as well as her strong connections with teachers, parents, and children over the years, were essential to this project—and to me personally. She was to be my bridge.[1]

Five months after that first visit, over lunch at my home, I asked her: "When we first started, what did you think the study was about?" Her reply was direct and sure, but, as I will make clear soon enough, she underestimated the extent of her role and her relationship to me and this study.

> MONIFA: Well, I took a look at your outline [my thesis proposal], and I thought you were trying to pull together some kind of investigation of children's games—outdoor games and building play spaces—and to refute the current theory that inner-city children don't use their imaginations in play; that they're pretty much involved in video games and that's about it. So, I was excited with the fact that you were refuting that.
>
> SALLY: And why did you think that was important?
>
> MONIFA: Ah, because of current theories about urban children and how they learn, and I think that a lot of misconceptions still persist about oppressed children and their learning abilities. And so, I thought that was important for that reason.
>
> SALLY: Why do you think I chose *you* for this?
>
> MONIFA: Oh, because we were friends, and you know that I'm an admirer.

---

1. I am grateful to Gladys Capella Noya for this term.

SALLY: And what did you think I wanted you to do?
MONIFA: Just provide children. Yeah, just provide a place to work, and children.

Monifa explained my study to school administrators, teachers, and parents. During my visit in April, she vacated her classroom so I might use it for interviewing children. Her assistance was also crucial in my locating children who built three-dimensional structures. When my interviews with 24 third graders revealed only two possible builders among them, she helped me find other candidates—partly by luck, partly through direct action. Allowing a group of fourth/fifth graders some free time to play following a nature walk near the school, Monifa overheard Michelle and Ayisha "playing house." She told me of her observation, and I interviewed the pair the next time I visited the school. Not counting on luck to produce possible candidates or my going to the fifth-grade classes to talk about my interest, Monifa asked three boys she knew well if they ever built anything. One did not, but in this way I met Michael and Rex.

In summary, I interviewed all the children who returned permission slips—30 in all. It may be that the children who did not return permission slips also build and play inside tents and teepees and, perhaps, even build clubhouses and treehouses. Additionally, it is likely that among the children who returned permission slips and were interviewed, I missed some who build structures because they did not recall past events, they chose to remain silent, they did not understand my questions, or they did not connect what they do with my questions. Eleven children—six boys and five girls—reported transforming spaces or building places, but only six corroborated their self-reports with photographs. Of the five not included here, three were boys who each reported building clubhouses outdoors, but before the study began, making on-site verification impossible. The two girls not included in the study each described setting up tents indoors, but one girl took photographs unrelated to the tent she described and the other started her tent-making only after playing in her friend Brenda's tent. (Mandy's tent differs from Brenda's in several ways: She uses a sheet instead of her bedspread; she varies the tent's location, sometimes setting it up in her bedroom as Brenda does, at other times in the living room; she builds on top of the bed or sofa instead of on the floor; and she uses her legs to hold the tent up instead of two chairs.)

WHERE THE CHILDREN LIVE

The children I came to know live and attend school in the neighborhood known as East Harlem in New York City, as explained in Chapter 1. My route to the school provided me with an extended view of the neighbor-hood. By foot and bus, I traveled up and down busy avenues, past candy stores, Chinese food take-outs and other small restaurants, laundromats, and, occasionally, a bank or pharmacy. I noticed that crisscrossing the avenues are quieter streets on which boarded-up buildings stand next to renovated ones, often with an evangelical church somewhere in between. In the mornings, I observed few kids outside playing, but the walk and view from the bus allowed me to observe the variation in housing and outdoor spaces from one block to another. Waiting for a bus in March, I caught snow flakes on my glove and shared their delicacy with a boy I didn't know, and one hot afternoon in June, I watched Brenda as she and other children waded in sneakers in the street in front of the school flooded by an open hydrant.

But always I was outside looking in. Only with the children's assistance did I begin to have an inside view of the apartments they call "home."

Home

Brenda, Michelle, and Ayisha live in "the projects"; Rex, Isaac, and Michael live in apartment buildings—one recently renovated, the other two built 10 and 40 years ago. The differences between the two are important.

"The projects," as they are called by residents, were built in East Harlem in the 1950s as part of a large-scale urban renewal program that replaced "tenements" in which, among other inconveniences, neighbors on the same floor often shared one bathroom. Rent for project tenants is based on need and subsidized by the state. The three buildings where the girls in this study live, plus the other buildings in the project, occupy four city blocks. In between the five- and seven-story buildings are parking lots, grassy areas divided by sidewalks, five small playgrounds, and two bas-ketball and handball courts. The school the children attend is located on the edge of the project.

Although the "projects" are apartment buildings, they differ in several respects from the buildings where Michael, Rex, and Isaac live. The latter were not, for instance, built on a mass scale with public funding. But the key difference is that the buildings where the boys live face streets and avenues. Hence, their outdoor play space is confined to sidewalks, stoops, alleys, and vacant lots. Isaac's building, for example, has a playground in the back, but he uses it rarely and never without his mother accompany-ing him. Michael lives on a busy street across from a large park where there are baseball fields, a swimming pool, and, at the far end, handball courts. Play in the street is dangerous, and he rarely goes to the park. Only Rex regularly plays outside. He describes his street as "down to earth; not like a lot of noise and things." My assumption was that children attending a "neighborhood" school shared a common physical environment—outside on city streets and inside their apartments. What I did not reckon on were how differently children experience the same city streets and to what extent family configurations might differ. I will explore each of these assumptions in turn.

To expect that one city street is like another or that an urban neighborhood is uniform or uniformly experienced was naive on my part. The following exchange between Isaac and Rick, both 8 years old, illustrates this point. The interview follows the two boys' making drawings of the places where they play. As they and I learn, Isaac plays mostly indoors, Rick plays mostly outdoors. Isaac explains the reason for playing indoors in terms of what he knows is outside, as follows:

SALLY: Okay, tell me why ONE[2] of you plays outside and ONE of you doesn't. Is it the same "outside"?

ISAAC: No. Not mine. 'Cause around my block there's a lot of shootings. And if you go outside there's actually someone who's going to steal something of yours or they're going to start a fight with you.

SALLY: Eiyee.

ISAAC: Or—

SALLY: But you live only six blocks apart!

ISAAC: I know. But it changes somewhere in between that my block is more dangerous than his.

This exchange took place early on in my interviews with the children; it made me reconsider my assumption that children experience and perceive a neighborhood similarly.

Regarding apartment interiors, I thought at first that what was most relevant were the types of buildings children lived in: an apartment in a tenement or in a housing project, for example. But what seems even more important are the people with whom children share the apartment (the number of people, their ages, gender, formal relationship to the child, as well as how they relate to the child). For example, Brenda has her own bedroom, but Isaac shares his with two older brothers. Table 2.1 shows four cases of children living with parent(s) and two with grandparent(s). Ayisha is the only child among adults.

---

2. Throughout, I capitalize words and syllables that the children (or in this case, I) said more loudly than others, assuming an intent to direct the listener's attention. To show that some words were drawn out—another way of signalling attention to a specific word— I use a hyphen, as in "bl-end."

Table 2.1 Children's family configurations, building types, and building locations

Child	Building type	Family configuration in addition to child participating in the study	Total
Brenda	Projects	Mother and one boy (a foster child)	3
Isaac	Apartment building (recent) on busy street	Mother, father, and 2 older brothers (older away during school year)	4–5
Ayisha	Projects	Grandparents, aunt, and 2 uncles	6
Michelle	Projects	Grandmother and 2 older cousins	4
Michael	Apartment building (prewar) on busy street	Mother, father, and one younger brother	4
Rex	Apartment building (renovated) on dead end street	Mother and an older brother	3

East Harlem, Separate and Unequal

Over 30 years ago, Covello (1958/1970) described this same community as an island separated from the rest of the city by both natural and cultural barriers: "Geographically, East Harlem is set apart from the larger city by definite natural boundaries on three sides, and on the south by a radical difference in the cultural composition" (p. 180).

In his description, Covello does not explicitly talk about economics. For Monifa, it is the key factor that limits the experiences of adults and children. She says:

A lot of children never get away from the community, not even as far as getting downtown . . . I can't generalize . . . but you know, even if they go to summer camp, it's a day camp. And they might have been taken out on field trips, but, if you're taken to Bear Mountain, you go to the swimming pool, you leave the swimming pool, you get on the bus, and you're back in the city.

I think about my growing up; it was very similar. I mean, we did take a Saturday excursion to Brooklyn or maybe we'd get on the ferry and go to Staten Island. But it took a long time before my father bought a car. He did send us one summer to a friend, who

lived in Port Jervis. It was his version of sending us away to camp
. . . It was a totally different experience for us to be in the country,
to walk to the lake and fish, and to walk into town where there was
a little general store. We were thrown into heaven—all the things
that we'd read in story books about kids in the country.

In saying she felt they were "thrown into heaven" that summer, Monifa
refers to the pleasures of nature, a sense of freedom, having fun, and the
seeming simplicity of country life. She is not alone. Indeed, in the chapters that follow, Michael claims that trees in the country are stronger than
trees in the city; Rex says kids can play on his street because it is "down to
earth"; and Brenda cuts off the lights, puts up her teepee, and pretends to
be in the woods camping out.

I will not discuss which is better, the city or the country. Neither will I
attempt to enumerate the limitations of growing up poor, as real, as important, and as unjust as these limitations are. Rather my focus is on how
city children go about remaking their world.

MOVING FROM OUTSIDER TO INSIDER

In my role as reseacher, I felt like an outsider. Monifa played a major role
in my moving from outsider to insider. In her mind, however, my even-
tual success owed little either to her efforts or to my conscious attempts to
fit in. Instead, for her, it was a matter of my being myself.

Outsider

I counted on Monifa to help me make sense of myself as researcher, but I
didn't wait to learn how she saw me; it was clear to me that because of
race and background, I was an "outsider" to the children's experience.

SALLY: The thing I want to explore next is my being an outsider.
MONIFA: Mm hmm.
SALLY: When I say that, I'm interested in what comes to mind for
     you.
MONIFA: An outsider? A person who doesn't live in the neighbor-
     hood. A white person from a different part of the country.
     Frankly, yeah, very different from, I mean, even very different
     from other whites that we interact with in the school system.
     The fact that you're not a New Yorker—and you NEVER come
     off as a native New Yorker: You'd never (*she laughs*) deceive

anyone. You could never say, "I grew up in, I was born and raised in—" No, no no, no (*she shakes her head, continuing to smile*).

SALLY: So how do you know? Accent?

MONIFA: Accent, your demeanor, the coloring.

SALLY: Uh huh.

MONIFA: I think the coloring.

SALLY: The coloring?

MONIFA: Yeah, your light hair, you know, the fairness of you. It's a very natural kind of look . . . It's unusual for native New Yorkers . . . there's a native New York look, I guess . . . yours must be the WASPISH look; I guess that's what it is.

SALLY: What?

MONIFA: As you said, you don't look Italian, you don't look Jewish, you don't—what are the other ethnic groups? You don't look like any Latino, definitely. You can't pass for black.

SALLY: Right (*we both laugh*). So, I'm a give-away? (*Monifa laughs.*) Okay, so in what ways do you think that—um, what's the effect of that?

MONIFA: Curiosity. Always curiosity.

SALLY: On the part of the kids?

MONIFA: Yeah, probably on the part of the kids.

SALLY: So it may not be something that puts them off?

MONIFA: No, I wouldn't think so. No. No, I didn't think. No, I don't think they would be put off. No, nor intimidated or, not at that young age, maybe older.

SALLY: Mm hmm.

MONIFA: And then, your demeanor's not officious, Sally; so you're not—maybe if you were an intimidating waspy-looking person, but your demeanor is very gentle. Not intimidating at all. The fact that you have the kids call you "Sally," and you blend in, you know.

SALLY: Even though I stand out—I'm tall (*we laugh*).

MONIFA: Your mannerisms are easy for you to blend right in. And it's interesting for me because when you sit in the classroom and you do the things that they do and you say, "Mrs. Wright," you know, it's not "Monifa," it's "Mrs. Wright." So just the terminology (*she pauses*). Which is interesting. Those are little fine points. I mean, how would you change it? I mean, if you came in all of a sudden one day and started, you know, calling me "Monifa" and you sat behind my desk, I mean, there would be a whole different body language, right? . . . And perhaps even your dress—a suit or high heels, stockings.

SALLY: I'd never be able to do that. . . . That must be what keeps me
   who I am (*we laugh*).

In the next section, I discuss in some detail ways I went about trying
to become an "insider." As Monifa observes in the above quotation, with
children, I "blend in"; it is within the adult world of the school that I felt
the "outsider." On the one hand, I was grateful for teachers' cooperation
and, in many instances, their friendliness; but, on the other, I felt uncomfortable in my dependence on their goodwill. I was sure that without their
assistance, I could not continue talking with the children. Hence, whereas
I found it easy to "blend in" with the children, I was often uneasy about
what it took to maintain the right balance among the adults.

Insider

During the spring and again in the fall of 1994, I was at the school for
1- to 3-day periods; in all, a total of 15 days. Typically, I arrived at 8:45 A.M.
and left at 3:30 P.M. Being on site over the school year and for 1–3 days
was necessary for several reasons. I needed time to establish my credibility with parents and teachers (children were more accepting). I needed
time to understand the rhythm of the school day if I was to interview
children without disrupting teachers' schedules. I needed time to become
reacquainted with a neighborhood I had known in the early 1970s when
I worked in a local boys' club and again in the late 1980s when, as an
educator in Central Park, I worked with children and teachers in local
schools.

In the mornings before school, I quickly stored my things in Monifa's
room and returned to wait outside for the morning bell. Often at this time,
younger kids stood with their parents, while older ones talked in twos and
threes or played tag on the sidewalk across the street from the school. When
the bell rang, children filed in and quickly formed long lines stretching
across the school gymnasium. Before and after the Pledge of Allegiance
and the singing of the national anthem, I greeted teachers and learned
what times might be more convenient for me to interview children.

At all times, I made it a point to know and speak to administrators,
teachers, and the security guards (one of whom, because she is on the
residents' board of the housing project, was very helpful in answering my
questions about the number of residents and what summer programs were
offered). I divided lunchtime between eating in the teachers' lounge and
being with the children, who played outside after eating lunch. When
eating lunch with the teachers, I nodded sympathetically when grievances

were discussed and expressed interest in the banter about current movies and upcoming weddings.

Being outside before school and during lunchtime allowed me to mingle informally with children who were part of my study. Equally important, I had opportunities to spend time with those children I had interviewed but whose play did not match my focus. In this way I could answer the question "Why haven't you talked to me again?" should it be asked. This was also an opportunity for me to watch what the children played in a semisupervised situation. I divided my time between the younger children (third grade and below), who had to play in a fenced-in area next to the school, and the older children, who were allowed to come and go, many playing games of chase and tag on project grounds across the street from the school, as others sat on benches, watching, eating, and talking.

When not interviewing children, I involved myself in school activities. In addition to being in line at the morning assembly, I attended a school talent show (Ayisha and Brenda danced to a popular song), and, with permission from the teacher of the combined fourth/fifth-grade classroom, I worked with children during two "activity periods" (my reasoning was that if children got to know me in this informal way, they would be more likely to want to talk with me and so return permission slips). And when Monifa needed another adult to help administer the citywide science test, I volunteered.

As during the morning routine, I was visible to children, parents, and teachers when school let out. Especially early on in my visits, I stood with Monifa on the sidewalk in front of the school; in this way I hoped to draw credibility from my proximity to her. She introduced me to parents of children who either had signed permission slips or might still do so. In addition, these times provided me with yet another opportunity to make contact with children I was interviewing, if only to say good-bye.

Thanking Teachers and Children

As the teachers gathered for lunch in June, I ceremoniously presented them with a cake and my sincere thanks for their cooperation and hospitality. During that same day, I invited the children I had videotaped to eat ice cream and cookies in Monifa's room as they watched excerpts of themselves on tape. As we finished up, I asked the children what they thought I might do next to learn more about children's play. The younger children (Brenda, for example) remained uncharacteristically quiet, but Michael was quick to recommend that I find out more about him—photograph him playing basketball, for example.

3 Collecting and Understanding the Material

In this chapter, I explain how I worked with the children and then how I went about trying to make sense of what they were telling me. More specifically, I first describe my three forms of data collection: interviews, drawings, and photographs. Then I discuss my qualitative methods of data analysis.

COLLECTING

I begin by describing the sequence and the content of my interviews with the children. I highlight the early phase of the process—what I call "getting acquainted"—and conclude with a brief dicussion of the reliability of children's self-reports. Next I present the second and third methods of data collection, children's drawings and photographs. With each, I describe in some detail the process of engaging children in the activity; I also pay particular attention to how I modified or changed the activity and how individual children solved problems that arose for them.

Interviews

The general structure of my data collection consisted of three to five open-ended interviews with each child. Beginning with more general questions about what they do and play, I followed with gradually more specific questions grounded in their responses (see Appendix B). Children's reactions to this approach were spontaneous, direct, and personal. Interviews were between 25 and 55 minutes in length over seven school visits, one to three days in length, in March, April, May, June, and November 1994.

Table 3.1 shows activities children engaged in at each session. The number of sessions with each child were as follows: three with Ayisha and Isaac; four with Michelle; and five with Brenda, Michael, and Rex. The fifth session took place after summer recess, and although I had looked forward to speaking with each child, three were either absent the day I visited or otherwise unavailable.

Getting Acquainted. In the first session with each child, I began by introducing myself as someone interested in what city kids do; I said not much was known and that's why I had come to them for answers. I said what they told me was private—which meant "just between us"; I added that I would not repeat what they said to their classroom teachers, parents, or classmates. I also said that if they didn't feel like saying something, they didn't have to—I wouldn't be upset—and that they could leave whenever they wished.

I told them that I would like to tape our interviews, showing them my micro-cassette recorder and how it worked. I explained that I would listen to our taped conversations on a machine I had bought especially for that purpose, typing up everything that was said. I explained that this was necessary in order to have as full a record as possible of our interview. If I didn't understand something, I said I would ask them the next time we met. Often the children turned the recorder on for me or, in some cases, got it working. In a later session, I explained that I would not use their real names in whatever I wrote and asked them to think of the name they wished to be called.

My intent was to establish and maintain a relationship with each child in which I was perceived as a nonjudgmental, curious adult who took them and their play seriously. No doubt all the children looked forward to getting out of class—something that carries some cachet in schools—but I also think, overall, the children felt appreciated and enjoyed telling me about themselves.

Table 3.1 Activities with children during interview sessions

Interview	Activity
Session 1	Drawing what they play and where; conversation and my questions about the drawing
Session 2	Reconsidering the drawing and planning the photographs
Session 3	Considering the photographs
Session 4	Reconsidering enlargements of some photographs
Session 5	Follow-up after the summer

Except for Michael and Rex, whom I interviewed separately from the start after they told Monifa they built things, my first interviews with children were in pairs. I did so initially for two reasons; a third reason for doing so became apparent during the process. First, I knew I would need to interview more children than the six I wanted for the study, and this seemed an efficient means to find builders. (I thought I would need to interview twelve to fifteen children to find the six; as it turned out, I needed to interview thirty.) Second, I thought most children—and third graders more than fifth—would feel more comfortable working with a strange adult if a classmate were present. (My assumption was that during subsequent interviews children, whatever their grade, would see me less as a stranger and therefore feel more comfortable. I was aware, however, that individual children would likely see me differently.) Third, in hearing the questions the children asked each other, I not only found out material pertinent to the study but also observed questioning techniques different from my own, some of which I subsequently tried.

Children's Self-Reports. While some might question the reliability of children's self-reports, my experience was compatible with Selltiz, Wrightsman, and Cook's (1976) assertion that only when children talk about their behaviors do adult researchers have opportunities to know what children do on their own. As documents of the particulars of children's experiences, both drawings and photographs provide something concrete—artifacts, if you will—that can be considered again and again. Consequently, by returning to the drawings and photographs at subsequent sessions, a fuller, richer, and more accurate description of what each child did, played, and built emerged. (To help me keep notes in a timely way, plan the subsequent interviews, and pay attention to what seemed important to each child, I made up a form I called my contact summary form and completed one following each interview; a copy is included in Appendix C.)

Drawing Activity

My second method of data collection—the drawing activity—was part of my first interviews with the children. I will discuss issues related to the drawing activity and some of the problems children experienced as they tried to draw what they play, where, and with whom. I will then describe what part the drawings played in subsequent interviews.

First Interview. In the first interview, I followed my introductory remarks by asking children to draw me a picture of what they played and where. I said the drawing could show what they play and do indoors or outdoors or both. If two children were present, I rearranged how they sat, often asking one child to move to a nearby table where I had already placed several sheets of white paper (11" by 17"), two sharpened pencils, and an eraser. By arranging the seating this way, I insured that each child's initial representation was not influenced by what the other drew.

I, too, could not see either child's work and consequently missed much of the sequence of their drawings. Watching to see if my interest made for inhibition, I would ask: Do you mind if I watch and take some notes? I did not want to appear to hover, as I thought this might distract the children from their efforts or put an evaluative edge to the enterprise. Hence, trying to look as if I were making notes about something else altogether, I jotted down what I did notice about drawing sequence as well as some descriptive material about each child.

For example, I observed Michelle draw and erase, draw and erase the same feature—namely, a peaked roof. Her erasures implied to me that it mattered to her to have a roof and perhaps a particular kind, as well. In her final version, however, the apex of the roof is not shown; it's off the page. But because I saw her make these erasures, I decided to listen especially for how she talked about the "roof."

Issues Related to the Drawing Activity. Only one boy, a third grader, said he did not want to draw. I said that was okay and excused him to return to class, and I continued with the second child who drew, then talked. Overall, the children seemed absorbed in the task. This is not to say, however, that all the children experienced drawing as easy to do. Because most of them seemed to assume my directions meant depicting specific people, familiar objects, and a particular place, they encountered real problems. These problems included drawing things in proportion to one another; showing distance; portraying movement; showing one thing in front of another; showing interiors as well as exteriors; conveying emotion; and drawing a straight edge when needed. Fifth graders Rex and Michael identify some of these common problems in the quotations that follow.

GETTING THE PROPORTIONS RIGHT

REX: This could be the coffee table. The coffee table is kind of bigger though.

MICHAEL: This is me-e-e. That's my little brother—I made him small (*he laughs*). These [two other figures] are me. It's hard to make them the same size.

GETTING THE DISTANCE BETWEEN THINGS RIGHT

REX: I made it [the TV] kind of far away. It's kind of like more probably like be right here.

SHOWING ONE THING IN FRONT OF ANOTHER

REX: So, this part of the fence. It's like over on this side of the building—past the garden. But I made it right here so you could see it.

When children looked up to say they were finished with their drawings, I moved to sit next to them. With the drawing between us, I said, "Please tell me about your picture." If the second child finished his or her drawing while I was talking to the first, I asked the first child if it was okay for the second to join us and, in addition, to ask questions if he or she had any. In every instance, the children agreed. They then switched roles when it was the second child's turn to talk about his or her drawing. Through this collaborative effort, I learned not only more about a particular drawing but what questions were okay to ask and how to ask them. (I will illustrate this last point in Chapter 5 about Isaac.)

Often as children talked about their drawings, they realized that important pieces of their story were missing. This was the case with Brenda. When I asked about the lights in her bedroom, she drew the missing light fixture; as she talked about the campfire scene, she drew a fork and marshmallow in one figure's hand; and as she talked about playing hide-and-seek inside her apartment, she drew her cousin standing behind a window curtain. Thus Brenda responded to my questions by saying more and drawing more.

Subsequent Interviews. After the first interview, I met with children individually. I had their drawings on the table in front of us. I asked both general and specific questions. For example, I asked Brenda to tell me more about what it looked like and felt like inside her teepee.

Second sessions varied both in their location and in how I recorded them. For example, on the first day of a four-day visit to their school in June, I learned that the second-grade teacher was away on a field trip. With a classroom available most of the day, I videotaped first Ayisha and then Michelle talking about their drawings. Ayisha taped her drawings together (she made two during the first session), fastened them to the chalkboard, and drew extensively on them with a marker; in contrast, Michelle helped me tape her drawings to the chalkboard but talked without referring to them. The next day, when a classroom was not available, I sat with Brenda at the end of a hall and audiotaped our conversation; videotaping it was impossible. On the third and fourth days of this same visit, I used Monifa's classroom when it was free. By quickly setting up and then taking down the video camera when Monifa needed the room, I videotaped conversations with both Michael and Rex.

Unlike the other five children, Isaac neither drew nor talked about building anything during our first conversation. However, I thought his play with GI Joes might lead somewhere. It did, but first I had to ask. My question was about potential building materials:

SALLY: Oh, I know, I wanted to ask you if you ever use your bed or sheets.

ISAAC: Yeah, I make it right here (*he points to bunk beds in his drawing*). I use 'em; I put them here.

SALLY: On the bunk bed?

ISAAC: Yeah, on the bunk bed and cover this part right here so I can make like a little house.

For the moment I will skip my third and fourth interviews with children, returning to them when I talk about the children's photographs; instead, I want to continue with the children's drawings and share a technique that came about quite by accident. Meeting with Brenda a fifth time, I began by saying I was writing up our earlier conversations and needed her help once more because I was still unsure about some things in her drawing. The dilemma was how to take note of her identifications but avoid changes in the original drawing. The solution was already at hand. Wanting to protect the children's drawings, I had placed each one between two pieces of acetate. Using an oil-based pencil, children could write directly onto the acetate and thus further elucidate their drawings yet not change the original.

Brenda went right to work. She seemed to enjoy both identifying features in her drawing and doing something different. Marks on acetate smear easily; after the interview, I copied her names for things onto a sketch I made of her drawing (a photocopy would work as well).

I conclude this section with Rex's remark. Referring to his drawing, he says, "[You have] to see it for yourself—it's hard to explain." I did not visit Rex's apartment and see for myself what he builds there. I was able, however, to see what he builds because of the photographs he took.

Photographs

I began this study undecided about using photographs as a method of data collection. The method was new to me and I thought the expense prohibitive. Once into the study, however, I saw more clearly why photographs of what the children built enriched the data; and just as important, I found a way to do it—give the children disposable cameras.

Photographs corroborate children's self-reports; they document a context; and, like the children's drawings, photographs can be considered over and over again. Photographs provide inventories of people, places, and things; views of the structure from different angles and perspectives; and the stages of the building process. Furthermore, taking photographs involves children themselves in the research process—they are on assignment.

Neither handling a camera nor having their pictures taken was new to any of the children. What was new for them was being asked to document an aspect of their everyday lives. To complete the assignment I gave them, children had to figure out how the camera worked, think about their options, identify and re-create the stages and the sequence of the building process, decide who should and should not be in a scene, manage family members, and so on.

I have divided the remainder of the discussion on photographs into four parts. The first outlines four basics of using photographs as a method of data collection. The second describes problems children encountered as photographers and how they solved them. Next I raise questions related to being the photographer and being the one photographed (some photographs being taken by the children, others by relatives and friends, and one set by me). I conclude with how I used the photographs in my interviews of the children.

Four Basics. Based on my experiences, the four basics for using photography as a method of data collection are (1) camera choice; (2) planning the assignment with the children; (3) getting the camera home; and (4) film processing. I will take each in turn.

1. *Camera choice*. I bought the cheapest disposable camera a store sold. The brand did not matter to me because there seemed little difference in the outcome. My only consideration was that the camera come with a built-in flash since I knew from talking with the children that they would be photographing indoors.

2. *Planning the assignment with the children*. I asked Brenda, Michael, Rex, and Isaac if they would like to use a disposable camera to document the structures they build. (For reasons I will explain later, I took the photographs of Ayisha and Michelle as they played outdoors.) I said I would like them to document both the sequence of the building process and the structure itself. In the following exchange, Brenda and I make a list of photographs she might take based on what she has previously told me about her play. Because her mother has signed a permission form, I assume it's okay for Brenda to photograph, but I check again and then we continue making the list:

SALLY: Is this going to be okay with your Mom?

BRENDA: Yeah. Take a picture inside of the outside and then take inside. And then I could probably go to the park where Mandy and I climbed a tree or something.

SALLY: Also, should you take a picture of the ghost? [Trying to scare cousin Catherine, Brenda turns a sheet over a chair into a ghost.]

BRENDA: Okay. What I could do is this: I could take a piece of paper and draw like the shadows—

SALLY: If there are shadows [made by light from her bedroom window or the flickering TV screen], take a picture; if not, don't worry about it. See where you get the best shots (*I stand on a chair to show her how to photograph from different heights*). And maybe one with ghost and the teepee.

BRENDA: Make this again? [Brenda refers here to the "campfire" she makes with a paper bag and colors the flames red with a crayon.]

SALLY: Oh, I know, when you start to make the teepee, stop and take a picture. You know how they show things that are "in progress"? Like stopping while cooking a cake.

BRENDA: Well, I'd show one with the sheet off, with the chairs tied together. Then I'd put the sheet on and take one.

SALLY: Okay, exactly, because having the sheet on you'd never know—(*Brenda interrupts*)

BRENDA: —how you built it.

SALLY: Exactly. Why don't you read what you've got so far on your list.

BRENDA: Teepee. Sit inside and take a picture of the outside. Take a picture of the ghost and fire. When you built it, take it of the chairs and the sheet.

SALLY: Great, great. I'll bring a camera tomorrow, and you'll check at home to see if it's okay?

BRENDA: Uh huh.

As promised, I gave a camera to Brenda the next day. She took it home, followed her list, and then brought the camera back. She gave it to Monifa, since I was no longer at the school and would not be on site for another two weeks. What happened to this camera remains a mystery, as Monifa could not find it when I returned. I immediately gave Brenda another camera. She soon brought it back. As it turned out, she remembered to photograph all but one of the items on her original list.

Two things seem critical for successful completion of this task: (1) children being clear about the purpose of the assignment (making a list with each child is helpful in this regard) and (2) children feeling that what is to be photographed and by whom is up to them. Only Rex photographed alone; the other children who took cameras home involved family members and friends both in taking the photographs and posing for them.

3. *Getting the camera home.* I placed the camera in a paper bag and instructed the children to keep the bag in their knapsacks for the rest of the school day. I explained that I wanted cameras to get home without mishap and that I did not want their classmates to feel slighted because they were not asked to take photographs, too.

4. *Film processing.* When cameras were returned, I took them to an East Harlem pharmacy for processing. On my walks to the pharmacy, I had opportunities to observe parts of the neighborhood new to me and, in turn, to be observed by residents. Processing was quick. During my June visits to the school, I left off cameras on the first day of my visit and picked up the prints on the third day. I paid for two sets of photographs, one for me and one set for each of the children.

Problems Children Encountered. The following examples illustrate the problems photographers Michael, Rex, and Brenda say they encountered and how they solved them. I have divided their experiences into the categories false starts, authenticity, and multiple perspectives.

In the quotation that follows, Michael recalls that first he needed to learn how to use the camera. After a false start (he mistakenly takes a photo of himself), he reads the directions written on the box and gets the camera to work.

It was a mistake. 'Cause I was trying to use the camera. That was like this—the flash. I had to read the instructions. So I pushed the flash. Click. Click. BUT, I got it to work.

Authenticity is an issue with Michael and one Brenda talks about as well. In Michael's case, the problem is how to show accurately where the crime takes place (in a bakery) in a typical episode of playing cops and robbers. With careful planning and the compliance of his younger brother, Allen, Michael solves this problem and others, as he explains next:

MICHAEL: It was a pain. I had to lock everybody out 'cause my brother wanted to come in. "Allen, you might get in the way of the picture." I had to go under my bed—the sides—because you wanted the view part.

SALLY: You locked everybody out?

MICHAEL: I had to lock the door and turn off the lights so it could look like we playing in the dark. And I took the Monopoly money—that's what we play with in the bakery. I put [the money] inside. I said, "Allen, I need you." "Why?" "I need you as a model, act like you stealing the money." He said, "All right." He act like he took the money, and I said: "Now get out of here." I took a lot of pictures.

SALLY: I gave you another set, right?

MICHAEL: Yeah. I got them at home.

Brenda, like Michael, enumerates the issues related to faithfully documenting what one plays, where, and with whom. When she and her younger cousin, Catherine, play house, Brenda plays the mother and Catherine, the teenage daughter. They pretend the closet in Brenda's bedroom is an elevator. (The elevator connects them to the world of school and stores that they pretend to visit.) In the quotation that follows, Brenda first acknowledges two common issues of documentation—completing the assignment and meeting the deadline. She follows by explaining the order in which photographs of the closet/elevator were taken.

Then this morning—'cause I said, "Sally wants the camera and everything," so I took it this morning. And Catherine—'cause we take Catherine to school—and Catherine was there, so Catherine got in the closet. And I closed the door all the way, and I took it. Then she stuck her head out, and I took it. So-oo that was about it.

A third issue raised by the children who took photographs is that of multiple perspectives. For Michael, the question is how to show the bakery from all sides. To do so, he crawls under his bed to photograph the structure of sheet and pillows from the rear. Rex is also interested in camera angles and views. He explains how he stood on a chair to achieve an aerial perspective of the three-dimensional structure he builds in his living room—he calls this view a "blimp mode," incorporating, I assume, his viewing of televised football games.

Does It Matter Who Takes the Shots? As I said earlier, I photographed Michelle and Ayisha one afternoon after school as they played outdoors. I took the set of photographs for three main reasons. First, I wanted to see for myself where these children played outdoors (in their case, a playground in "the projects"). A camera, I thought, lent credibility to my role as a researcher/reporter. Second, I took the pictures, rather than either Michelle or Ayisha, because I wanted them to be in them—to be playing. Third, the loss of Brenda's camera was a setback in terms of time. It was now mid-May, and I reasoned that if I used the camera now I would be sure to have photographs when I returned in June. With these considerations in mind, I arranged to meet Michelle and Ayisha the next afternoon. In the meantime, they were supposed to tell their families what we were doing and when.

Monifa accompanied us. It's a very short walk from the school to the playground where Ayisha and Michelle play. Once there, I proposed starting with a group shot and motioned Michelle, Ayisha, and Monifa to a bench where they were to sit. As I backed off to take the picture, the "group," to my surprise, got larger. The photograph I finally took shows Monifa sitting with Michelle and Ayisha and their three girlfriends. Seemingly out of thin air, the players had all appeared.

As the girls played on the climbing tower, I walked around photographing them. I then asked if we could go to the tree where they once had built a clubhouse, as reported by both girls in our first interview. Michelle and Ayisha led the way from the playground to one corner of the housing development. There I photographed them among the branches of the crabapple tree. Before leaving, Ayisha pointed out to me her apartment in the building nearby; it overlooks the tree.

It does matter who does the drawing. But in what ways and to what extent does it matter who takes the photograph, frames the shot, chooses the perspective? In other words, does it matter if the child is in the picture or not, behind the camera or not? Both photographers will illustrate aspects of the work, but you learn different things. Brenda, for instance, is in some photos and not others. Whether she is in front of the camera or behind, she looks posed. Aware of the camera, she smiles. In the case of Michelle and Ayisha, I framed each shot and decided on what to shoot and when. Nonetheless, the girls talk about the photographs in vivid detail. Here, for example, is Michelle talking:

Well, this is the picture where we play house at. You see where is me, Munchkin, Leontye, and Mika. We always playing house.

And we telling the little boy Anthony, we was telling him. We act like we tell him to get ready for school: "Go wash up" and "It's time to wake up."

Michelle and Ayisha were playing as I photographed them, and the photographs catch them in action. They are not facing the camera; instead, their bodies are turned toward each other. One consequence is that, although they were reconstructing their play for me, their gestures appear more spontaneous than those of Brenda and her friends.

Rex and Michael present a different angle because they are the sole documenters of their play and what they build. One consequence is that, except for Michael's photograph of his face—a mistake—we do not see how they position themselves inside the structures they build.

Finally, as said earlier, Isaac's case is different because his mother took all the shots. I learned what her experience as observer/photographer meant for her in a conversation I videotaped in June. It happened by accident: Being told Isaac was absent from school, I found his mother (she worked in the school, assisting in one of the kindergarten classrooms) and asked her to take home his set of photographs. As we looked at them together, she said: "It surprised me so much. . . . I really learned so much about him in these few pictures that I took. It was great . . . he taught me about himself."

Like Isaac's mother, I also learned a lot. From children's talk, drawings, and photographs, they taught me about themselves. To complete this section on methods of data collection, I explain next how I used the photographs with the children.

Method. I numbered each photograph, writing on the back. In this way, when children referred to a photograph, I asked them to say its number, and I could be sure I was looking at the same photograph when later I read the interview transcript.

During the time of data collection, I took a course at the Harvard Graduate School of Education in visual ethnography taught by Catherine Krupnick. Krupnick insisted that class members keep each other up to date on their efforts. In May, just before I was to talk for the first time with children about their photographs, Irene Hall, a fellow student, made what turned out to be a timely suggestion about method. It was based on a mistake, she informed us. By asking specific questions rather than more open-ended ones, she thought she had too narrowly confined children's responses and thus missed knowing what they thought important.

Hall's advice matched my sense of what was appropriate and effective; it was similar to how I asked children to talk about their drawings. I made a slight change, however. Because there were 12 to 15 photographs in contrast to one or two drawings, my method was to ask children to choose from among the photographs those they wanted to talk about.

Also, at Krupnick's suggestion, I selected one to two photographs from each child's set and had photocopied enlargements made. The basis of my selection varied with each child. For example, with Ayisha and Michelle in mind, I chose clear pictures of the climbing tower where they play house and the crabapple tree where they built a clubhouse. I expected some repetition and some elaboration. In preparation for a fourth session with Isaac, for example, I enlarged the photo showing the interior of the little house he makes using his bunk beds. My hope was that he would say more about the stuffed animals that are on a shelf in the background.

As it turned out, I used enlargements of specific photographs as the focal point of my fourth interviews only with Brenda and Michelle. For the most part, Brenda and Michelle repeated what they had said before. This method corroborated children's earlier descriptions but provided little elaboration. I felt the outcome might be different with Isaac. But his absence from school prevented me from showing him an enlarged version of the toys he plays with in what he calls his "little house."

Enlargements of photographs do not necessarily make anything clearer, but they do involve children and the adult researcher looking again and so offer the possibility that something missed will now be noticed.

UNDERSTANDING

I used qualitative methods for data analysis. In the discussion that follows, I have divided the methods into text, drawings, and photographs to explain each in greater depth. However, the separation of one method from another does not adequately represent the dynamic, concurrent quality of the analytic process as I experienced it; namely, the way my thoughts and questions emerged and evolved over time. As I wrote in a memo to myself in January 1995: "There's a lot to be said for letting the material tickle me, look me in the eye, knock me over the head. To let that happen, I turn to it again and again."

Analysis began during data collection. Before subsequent interviews with each child, I reviewed contact summaries (see Appendix C for the format I used for making notes after every contact) and listened to the audiotape of our previous interview. As I listened to tapes or viewed videos, I noted segments I wanted clarified and directions I hoped to pursue. When I wanted to capture an idea or feeling, I wrote a memo. In a similar fashion, when coding the interviews and while considering the drawings and photographs, I made notes and wrote memos. In these ways, analysis was ongoing and iterative.

Analysis of Children's Words

I use *text* here to mean transcribed interviews, notes, memos, and journal entries. My methods for analyzing text were as follows:

- Listening to children talk about what they do and play; listening again to the audiotapes of these sessions, listening *and* watching them on video. Two children were filmed once; four, twice.
- Transcribing the taped interviews. Sessions that were videotaped were later audiotaped and transcribed.
- Reviewing videotaped sessions to add children's gestures to the transcript.
- Creating a "play summary." A play summary is a matrix for recording and displaying children's descriptions of their play in general and their "worldmaking" activities in particular. It organizes each activity according to its location, props used, and players—by gender, age, and group size.
- Coding the transcripts to identify themes that children express as important to their experience. Themes I identified from this process include "know-how," "scary," "peers—relationship," and "adult work." Transcripts were in two forms—hard copy and computer files. I coded the material at least twice: manually on hard copies of the transcripts and using the software program HyperRESEARCH.
- Coding memos and journal entries to identify themes. As I worked, I added new codes to my list (e.g., "light and darkness," "animals," and "photography—explanations"). I used the commercial software program HyperRESEARCH for coding typed materials; I coded any handwritten material manually (e.g., journal entries I had not typed).
- Organizing material. I created a notebook for each child that consisted of contact summaries, transcribed interviews, drawing summary, and coded material. I arranged the latter in alphabetical order according to the code name. A hierarchy of code names further helped to make the material accessible for analysis. For instance, "structure" was a major category but too all-encompassing as a code; yet, I did not want to lose data connected to it. My solution was to create a subset of codes all starting with "structure." (In HyperRESEARCH, themes are shown in alphabetical order; hence, all those starting with "structure" appear together.) Three examples will illustrate my point: "structure—origins," "structure—description," and "structure—materials used."

Analysis of Children's Drawings

Analysis of children's drawings and maps is not new to research on children's play (Hart, 1979; Ladd, 1970, 1972; Sobel, 1993). Unlike others, however, I was interested neither in counting up "elements" and organizing them into categories nor in speculating on which drawing shows which child to be more competent than another (Mauer & Baxter, 1972; R. C. Moore, 1980). In contrast, I conceived of children's drawings as a second medium for capturing children's understanding of interactions and relationships with their environment.

To analyze children's drawings of places where they play and what they play, I developed a drawing summary form (see Appendix D) based on Brenda Engel's work (1991) on portfolio assessment. As developed by Engel, a drawing is considered according to six descriptive characteristics, as follows: materials and setting, basic elements and techniques, genre, meaning and organization, what it involves or represents, and its sources. Each of these descriptors is reflected in my drawing summary.

Under Engel's direction, I tried out the summary on a child's drawing from my pilot study and, based on this experience, I made revisions. During several practice sessions that followed with children's drawings from my pilot study, I realized that I was not following the format but, instead, starting by asking myself, "What do I notice?" Although the results looked interesting, it seemed to me that aspects of the drawing summary were not being attended to in full. In fact, it seemed more difficult to think about shapes and organization, for example, once I had in my mind what the drawing represented for me.[1] Hence, after these early explorations, I returned to the drawing summary and faithfully followed its order.

A second change is important to note. After considering Brenda's drawing on my own, I invited two to three people to join me in looking at a child's drawing. At these times I remained silent about what information I had (e.g., that Isaac's drawing represented his bedroom). I either typed responses onto the format as people talked or taped the sessions, then filled in the format. In this way, I was open to others' perspectives that might challenge my own.

In the chapters that follow, each child's drawing is displayed and analyzed. But how they are woven into the text varies from one child to another. For example, in the chapter about Isaac, I open with his drawing. At this point, I purposely present little explanation or interpretation about either the drawing or the drawer. Instead, I present excerpts from the drawing summary and follow with questions put to Isaac by his classmate, Rick. Only then do we hear from Isaac.

I have several intentions here. First, I want readers to consider Isaac's drawing on its own—from their point of view. Second, I want to convey the difficulty in understanding not only what is there but also what Isaac

---

1. I am appreciative of Ellen Doris, who encouraged me to follow the format.

intended. And third, I want to suggest that multiple points of view enrich our understanding and help keep it complex.

Analysis of Photographs

Photographs contributed to this study in three main ways: (1) They stimulated children's descriptions of what they build and play; (2) they corroborated children's self-reports; and (3) they allowed children considerable autonomy as expert and decisionmaker about personal, sometimes private behaviors.

The photographs show how accurate the children were in depicting the spaces where they play. Both Brenda's and Rex's photographs are excellent illustrations of this point. Because Brenda reconstructed and then photographed her teepee in its usual location, I understood better how it is possible for her to use natural light from a nearby window to create shadows. By reconstructing and then photographing from different distances and angles the structure he makes, Rex helped me better understand its relation to other furniture in the family's living room.

PART II

Six Worldmakers

The five chapters that follow form the core of this book: Six children, three boys and three girls, 8 to 12 years old, describe the three-dimensional structures they build in city apartments and on city playgrounds and sidewalks. To make these constructions, the children use what's available—materials such as bedcovers, pillows, and cardboard, for example. They also use knowledge based in family, school, and popular culture. Alone and with peers, the children shape this mix, adding to it their wishes and visions. Inside their teepees and clubhouses, their tents and playhouses, the children seclude themselves from the rest of the world; there they find room to experiment and permission to re-write who they can be in a world often closed to them.

I knocked and was allowed inside. Intentionally, I entered not as a tourist, but as a guest, appreciative and open to possibility. As you listen to the children's stories that follow, I invite you to do the same.

4 BRENDA:
Sojourn in a Dark Wood

B renda finishes her drawing, puts down her pencil, and looks up. I move to sit next to her, the drawing between us (see Figure 4.1). Brenda will add to her drawing as she recalls other inside play activities,[1] but for now, creating a teepee is central (she uses "teepee" and "tent" interchangeably). Brenda tells me:

> Well, here I got the two chairs with my cousin and me under; it's like a teepee. . . . And here's my bed for like my room. And we're under there watching TV, and we like to play under there and stuff. So that's how we make the teepee—'cause we put the two chairs together and the sheet over it and lift up the sheet on top of the chairs so we could see. And we watch TV, eat potato chips and have fun—like if we really camping.

With this passage, Brenda provides a concise summary of how she builds the teepee, its location, what she and her cousin play, what they eat and do, and her name for this activity—camping.

After this first meeting, I write in my notes: "Brenda's voice is strong; she seems sure of herself, and solid physically and in her presentation of self." This perception persists whether we talk more formally or greet each other before and after school. "She smiles," "She laughs," "She giggles," and "We both laugh" are recurring phrases in the transcripts, conveying Brenda's ease and delight with the world both as she experiences it and as she pretends it to be.

---

1. In order to display Brenda's drawing as it appeared at this point in our conversation, I carefully deleted material she added as we talked. The "finished" drawing is shown later in this chapter (see Figure 4.2).

Figure 4.1. Brenda's Early Drawing

This chapter continues with a description of Brenda's home arrangements, her playmates, and their play indoors. Next I review what Brenda does and plays outdoors so as to compare outdoor to indoor play. Both the indoor activities in her bedroom and the outdoor activities in playgrounds are restricted, even limited, yet what she does indoors comes across as imaginative and fun for her, a puzzle I will consider. In the last part of this chapter, I return to Brenda's teepee-building, its origins, what she does when inside, and the meanings she gives to her play.

HOME ARRANGEMENTS AND PLAYMATES

Brenda lives in public housing with her mother and a 2-year-old boy she calls "baby brother"; he is a foster child. Her photographs, taken either by Brenda, her aunt, or her best friend, Mandy, show that the space she calls her playroom is filled to overflowing (the word *stuffed* comes readily to mind) with furniture, objects, and has a color scheme (pink and white).

The photographs also show an attentiveness to what Brenda likes— dogs. A poster of a dog hangs on the wall; dogs are the motif on window curtains and pillows as well as in her play. Brenda announced to me that she hopes to get a puppy because, as she said, "I always wanted a dog since I was 4. I've been bugging my mom." Until then, she brings an object into the teepee that is soft like the puppy she wants. She explains: "Sometimes I bring a blanket for me and Catherine to share—or just me to share. And I bring my/my favorite pillow—dogs."

A Younger Cousin

In the past, Brenda played exclusively at home with her cousin Catherine, a second grader at the school where Brenda is a third grader. In the passage below, Brenda explains that teepee-building began a year ago as something she taught Catherine:

> Well my cousin was in the first grade and I was in second—in Mrs. Lefkowitz's room [pseudonym]. So when my cousin came over I thought (*she pauses*) 'cause Ms. Lefkowitz had said you could put two chairs together—and put a sheet over. So I thought maybe I should [make this] with my cousin.
> So we took two chairs—tied 'em/tied 'em at the end. So then we put a blanket over them and we went inside. So we put on the side where my TV was right there, and I was watching TV with her.

In later conversations, Brenda expresses her mixed feelings about her cousin. On the one hand, Catherine is available as a playmate and, because she is a year younger, plays the part of the daughter when they play house. But theirs is also a forced association and, in the sequence that follows, Brenda confides the direct action she took one afternoon to make Catherine go home during a game of hide-and-seek. Brenda's manipulation of light and dark is a point I return to later when discussing her teepee play.

> And Catherine's father came—and she hates going home—she likes staying in my house. So what she does is, "Brenda, you hide me, I don't want to go" (*she whines*). I be like: "You have to go." Because sometimes I don't like her too much because she's stubborn and she's very bad. She's mean to my mother and I don't like that.
> Then my mom came in and said, "Where's Catherine?" And I said, "Hiding somewhere, I don't know." So then when my Mom left I went out of the room 'cause I really want her to go home. So what I did was, I turned off the light, closed the door. She got scared and run out (*she giggles*). She ran from under the bed and ran to her father crying 'cause she got scared. Finally she went home.

As mistress of the lightswitch, Brenda manipulates the environment in which she plays. As we will see, using darkness and shadows to create a "spooky" surround is essential to how Brenda makes teepee play "like . . . REALly camping out," a point she emphasizes by accenting the first syllable.

A New Friend

In my second interview with Brenda, a new playmate is introduced—a fellow third grader named Mandy. The discussion exposes the differences in Brenda's relationships, reveals what being best friends means for her, and provides information about how someone new is brought inside the teepee.

Interestingly, during our first conversation, Brenda had not mentioned Mandy. Nor is Mandy one of the figures in her drawing. It is not until we talk a month later that she tells me the change and explains how Mandy became her best friend:

> I had a best friend—I had three best friends—and Mandy's one of them. But then Tabitha, this other friend I had, she moved to another school. Then, one friend I had, Ashley, she moved to another school. So Mandy's the only one I have.

Our third conversation takes place 2 months later. At that time, Brenda reports a change in intensity in her friendship with Mandy as evidenced in that they now "go to each other's house every single day"; this turn-taking, she explains, is a matter of degree of a friendship.

> Soooo, now we are best friends: We go to each other's house—every single day—and we have lots of fun (*she smiles*). Me and Tabitha didn't really go to each other's house—we weren't that good of friends—so we could go to each other's house every single day (*she laughs*). We're with each other every single day: from eight-thirty to like six. Because we're all day we're in school we're together. Then I go to her house from three to six. Then she goes to my house from three to six.

During this period of evolving friendship, Brenda makes room for Mandy in her teepee. Additionally, room is made for "baby brother." Brenda begins by explaining how it used to be; that is, just Catherine and herself:

And we might be side by side to watch the TV or something; and/ but in the meanwhile, we might be watching scary stories and everything. So, when Mandy comes over, she's in the middle—near the entrance—so we have enough room. And my baby brother wants to join us (*she laughs*) so we have all four of us in there.

OUTDOOR PLAY

Outdoors, as indoors, Brenda usually plays with Catherine. Brenda says she rides her bike and Catherine roller-blades. The sidewalks of the housing project where Brenda lives are their boundaries, and the girls are always supervised by one of their mothers.

> Sooo, sometimes Catherine's mother, (*gives her first name*), she takes us outside. We ride bikes, and (*she sighs*) I love to ride bike—or scooter—and stuff. And Catherine has roller skates.

Following the above quotation, Brenda shares two memories with me. The events are similar in that each conveys her delight in experiencing natural phenomena. Additionally, in her retelling, we glimpse feelings of novelty, spontaneity, and mastery.

Just the day before our conversation, she and other children had played in a manmade river. School was out, and adults had opened two hydrants (sometimes called pumps), flooding the dead-end street that runs between the projects and the school. (In her car, Monifa and I made our way through the "river" as we left the school that day.) Brenda tells me straight off about what it felt like getting "wet in the pump":

BRENDA: I went over there yesterday and we got soaked.
SALLY: It looked like fun.
BRENDA: Yeah, it was—but that was CO-LD water. Soooo there were a whole bunch of kids over there.

The second memory Brenda relates is her visit in early spring to Central Park with her best friend Mandy, Mandy's two boy cousins (one of whom, Wayne, is in their class), and Mandy's father. Among other things, they climbed trees:

BRENDA: It was my first time.
SALLY: Your first time? [I am genuinely surprised and then awed.]
Did Mandy know how to do it? How did YOU learn?

BRENDA: No. Wayne knew how to do it.[2] So he just told us what to
do and we got up. He went ALL the way up in the tree and we
just half way up . . . So I made this vow to climb the tree (*she
laughs*).

SALLY: And how did you feel afterwards?

BRENDA: We-ll (*she draws out the word*), I want to go back and climb
the tree. It was fun. We like climbed like two or three trees.

Brenda's recollection of tree-climbing shows her determination. As she
put it, she made a "vow to climb the tree." I am sure she also made a silent promise to return and climb again. Like other city children, both boys
and girls, she must rely on adults first to create an environment that includes trees—lots of them of all different sizes, shapes, and ages—and then
to take children to where the trees are.

INDOOR PLAY

In this section, I consider the similarities and differences between and
among three activities Brenda plays indoors. The activities are hide-and-
seek, playing house, and camping. Each is interesting as an example of
Brenda's creative play, but of particular interest are the ways in which
camping—the play in which Brenda builds a three-dimensional structure—
differs from playing hide-and-seek and playing house.

Hide-and-Seek

Hide-and-seek can be a lively game, partly because it often includes a chase.
But the size of Brenda's apartment curtails such expanded physical activity. When she plays, Brenda depends on deception and the knowledge that
she knows something her cousin does not. In addition, and more in the
spirit of collaboration, the girls find a variety of ways to keep the game
satisfactory for both of them.

BRENDA: So, that's one of the things me and my cousin do (*she
pauses*). And what we really like to do is play hide-and-seek. And
where I where I mostly hide is in the closet in my room (*she

---

2. I asked Brenda why she thought Wayne knew how to climb trees. She said: "Maybe/
maybe since he was a boy, he did um he climbed the tree because um, sort of like boys are
more hyper (*she laughs and me, too*). Because most of the boys like to climb trees and do
other things. So the girls, we didn't hardly know how to climb trees."

pauses to draw a slim rectangle in the lower-right-hand corner;
see Figure 4.2). When I hide in there sometimes (*she chuckles*),
Catherine can't find me too well.

SALLY: How come?

BRENDA: Because I get very INside of the closet 'cause the closet's
like a big room, so what you have to do is sometimes I go in
there and hide myself in the clothes (*as if to emphasize where she*
hides, she adds a clothes hanger hooked over a rack).

SALLY: Oh, and she thinks you're just clothes.

BRENDA: Yes, she'll never know.

SALLY: Clever, clever.

Catherine's usual hiding place is behind curtains. Brenda draws
Catherine behind the curtains in front of a window in the upper-right-
hand corner of her drawing (refer to Figure 4.2). She then continues.

BRENDA: Where/where she likes to hide is in my baby brother's
room. She likes to hide in the window 'cause she hides herself/
she hides herself in the window/in the, the—

Figure 4.2. Brenda's Finished Drawing

SALLY: Curtains?

BRENDA: Curtains.

SALLY: Ah, clever.

BRENDA: She hides herself there. So when/with the curtains over her, sometimes I don't see her. If it's night, I don't see her. But morning I could see her because I see her shadow.

SALLY: Oh, she doesn't realize about the light. You're tricky (*Brenda smiles*).

The girls attempt to vary this game. Brenda explains that sometimes the one who hides first records on a piece of paper where she will hide; she hides the paper and then goes to the hiding place (writing and hiding take place as the seeker counts from 1 to 25 with eyes closed). This variation not only helps to prolong the game but also makes it more challenging as a piece of paper is easier to hide and more difficult to find than a person.

Playing House

Of the indoor activities she describes to me, Brenda likes playing house the least. Her lack of enthusiasm may be due, in part, to its being her cousin's idea. Moreover, the play does seem tiring as described here—it lacks what Brenda calls "spookiness" and I would call drama.

BRENDA: My cousin she always like playing house. I don't like it that much 'cause I get tired of it. Well, I would be the mother, she would be the daughter; we use the dolls also. I have a life-sized Barbie, and we would play with her, too, like she the neighbor or something.

SALLY: Where do you play house?

BRENDA: In my house.

SALLY: Which room or rooms?

BRENDA: My room. We do all different things in my room. But my room's not actually my room—it's a playroom.

SALLY: This is the playroom, right? (*I point to Figure 4.2*)

BRENDA: Yeah.

SALLY: So which part of the playroom do you usually play house?

BRENDA: Well, we would go around the room and the closet right here (*she points to lower-right-hand corner*), we pretend it's a house—my life-sized Barbie's house.

Abruptly, Brenda shifts our discussion away from playing house and brings it back to hide-and-seek. She concludes by saying that her preferred play is neither playing house nor the game hide-and-seek, but rather "doing those tents."

> Sometimes when we play hide-and-go seek . . . I sometimes hide in the closet or behind the couch. So we have a lot of fun in it, but the most fun we have is doing those tents.

"Doing Those Tents" and Teepees

With the words, "Well, here I got," Brenda quickly directs my attention to her drawing, a detail of which is shown in Figure 4.3. She first points out to me the "two chairs" placed back to back and then the two figures standing side by side. The girls look a lot alike: they wear similar long tops that have no necklines over similar long pants; they have long hair and bangs and they are smiling. Moreover, the left hand of each is partially hidden

Figure 4.3. Two Campers

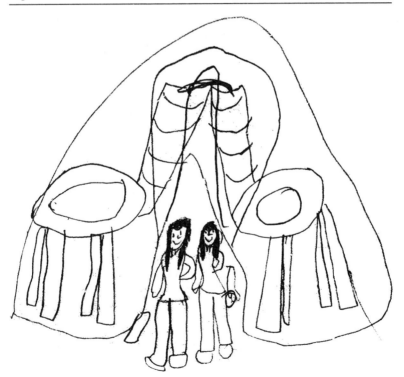

behind the figure's back or, perhaps, resting on her respective hip. However, what seem to be identical twins are slightly different in height and in head shape: the figure on the right is shorter than the one on the left and, as might be expected, has a smaller head; unexpectedly, the smaller head is differently shaped—more rounded than the head of girl on the left. These reflections come later, when I have time to look closely. Assuming that taller is equal to "older" in Brenda's eyes, I ask Brenda the next time we talk if she is the girl on the left and her cousin, the girl on the right. She confirms my assumptions.

Both figures seem dwarfed by the chairs (this may be partly because Brenda drew the teepee first, then added the figures). If I squint my eyes, the chairs appear as a pair of four-legged, long-necked creatures, their heads touching at a point high above the figures.[3] The effect, whether they are chairs or my imagined creatures, is that of a monumental arch under which two girls stand, side by side, their happy faces turned outward. In fact, they are under something—as Brenda explains, "it's like a teepee."

Getting Started. I expected more of a flow between indoor play activities; for example, hide-and-seek becoming teepee-building, all in the same afternoon. But Brenda keeps them separate, as she explains in the passage that follows. Also here, she tells how first she, and then Catherine, learned about teepees from their second-grade teacher, Mrs. Lefkowitz:

SALLY: How do you tell Catherine you want to do the tent or teepee? Like, what do you say?

BRENDA: WELL, when I tell her I be like, "You want to play a game?" And she says, "Okay." But like, "You want to do something?" She says, "Okay." And I tell her, "You want to make a tent?" And she says, "Great," 'cause she loves making a tent.

SALLY: Oh. Whose idea was it in the first place?

BRENDA: Mines (*she pauses*). So what she does—she already know how to make a tent because she's in Mrs. Lefkowitz's class [now]. 'Cause Mrs. Lefkowitz—that's the way I knew how to make a tent. Because she [Ms. Lefkowitz] took two sticks—and she told us we could make it with chairs if we want. So she takes two sticks: She puts like BIG brown paper around it and then, one by one, the whole class gets under.

---

3. Dr. Leah Levinger, psychologist and professor at Bank Street College of Education, imparted this hint about squinting. I found that, for me, squinting helped concentrate my attention on specific features of the drawing rather than the whole.

SALLY: Really? (*Brenda makes a sound that makes me feel that she is happy in thinking about this experience; her next words confirm my thinking.*)

BRENDA: We had fun. That's why I want to make it (*she pauses*). And we have a lot of fun making a tent. Like if you are camping out.

Influences. When we talk in June, I ask Brenda to say more about her earliest teepee-building experiences. In the passage below, she recalls how she used a school experience to guide her:

> We-ll my cousin was in the first grade and I was in second—in Mrs. Lefkowitz's room. So when my cousin came over, I thought (*she pauses*) 'cause Mrs. Lefkowitz had said you could put two chairs together and put a sheet over. So I thought maybe I should with my cousin.
>
> So we/we took two chairs, tied 'em/tied 'em at the end. So then we put a blanket over them and we went inside. So we put on the side where my TV was right there, and I was watching TV with her.

Brenda has not been to summer camp but has camped out with her family; particular aspects of the experience are recalled below, with keen attention to the creepiness of night as opposed to a picnic on "nice grass" in the morning.

BRENDA: In this place where you go to picnic—a picnic place—where there's nobody and when it's dark—it's like creepy.

SALLY: You did this with your family?

BRENDA: Yes. Once. And um it's nice when you go on a picnic in the morning because there's nice grass. You could bring your bike or anything . . . and you be with your family.

"Like If It's Real." Brenda's conviction that her play feels real to her comes as a surprise to me. Is she kidding? Two chairs covered by a sheet in a bedroom is "like if we REALly camping"? Brenda is confident insofar that Catherine feels like they are really camping. She gives this reason: "And since Catherine's never been camping, what happens is, that I do that, and when she gets in she feels like she's in the real thing." Catherine knows from observation how to dress up to look like a teenager when they play house, but knowing little about camping except from vicarious experiences—watching television, reading stories, and going to movies—she relies on Brenda for authenticity.

Brenda is aware of the responsibility to make the scene scary so it "be like it is real," the phrase she uses to begin the next passage: "I turn off the lights. I take some food in, and I stay there with Catherine, talking. We say creepy stories . . . And it's real dark and we watching TV. Having fun. So we really like it—doing that." Darkness, food, being scared are the ingredients to staging a successful camping out. In addition, she includes the traditional campfire and marshmallows: "We pretend we have camp-fires. Instead of having a stick to put the marshmallow on, we usually have a spoon (*she laughs as she says this*)."

But it's not just Catherine for whom camping seems real—it's real to Brenda as well. Essential to making camping real, Brenda informs me, is imagining you are some place else: "BUT, what I/what I make it is: I just pretend that I'm NOT in the bedroom, that I'm outside." At another time, she returns to this point, saying: "We like pretending like if it's real—our imaginations. . . . And we pretend we're IN it."

Taking the role of stage manager, Brenda is responsible for the set, the props, and special effects. She even uses what can be seen from the window to create the scene she wants: The tree framed by the bedroom window helps convince Catherine she is outside. "Sometimes when it's night, we turn off the light—there's no light at all. So we have like a flashlight. And right here there be a shadow of a tree."

As this quotation and the others suggest, most important is the atmo-sphere—physical and psychological—created around the teepee. For an example, Brenda explains, "We try to make it real spooky." To create this spookiness, the girls read, tell, or watch scary stories and Brenda makes things bump the teepee! The wind blowing in from an open window and shadows created by the TV remind both girls of ghosts—but only one of them gets scared. And just to make sure, Brenda puts an old blanket on a chair and tells Catherine it's a ghost:

> BRENDA: Well, when I'm in the tent, I sort of pretend that it's a
> scar-y night in the woods with a teepee there. And I tell her
> scary stories. And she get really really scared. So what I would do
> is—'cause you know how make it—like in the woods and stuff. I
> move a lot of things near the tent and I shut off the lights. We're
> under there [the teepee] and we see the spooky shadows. She
> thinks it's like a ghost, and she real scared.
>
> SALLY: But how can she see the shadows if she's underneath the tent?
>
> BRENDA: Because the blanket is a see-through blanket—kinda you
> could see through it. She sees the shadows and she gets scared. . . .
> And I'd be like, "Catherine, look." And she's be like "Oooooh" and
> holding me tight.

With Brenda's help, I have identified the features she uses to create the spooky atmosphere around the teepee and labeled them on her drawing (see Figure 4.4).

I ask Brenda why *she* never gets scared but Catherine always does. She confirms my hunch that being the authority-in-residence and taking charge of the production gives her a different view of the situation. She says: "Yeah, because I'm the one who does it." On the other hand, teepee life is not only about being scared, even for Catherine—there's eating popcorn or potato chips and there's pretending to roast marshmallows. Then again, really camping *is* a bit scary in that you are on unfamiliar ground; the sounds may be strange to you and, if you stay, it's going to get dark.

Figure 4.4. Brenda's Drawing with Selected Features Identified

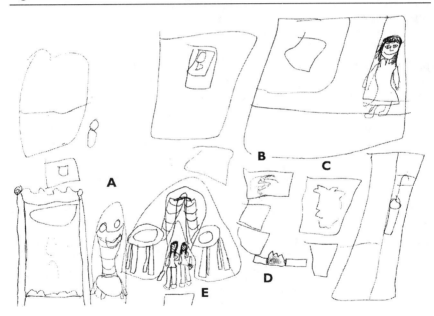

A   Ghost
B   Tree's shadow
C   Tree outside window
D   Campfire
E   TV

In a later conversation (our fourth), I learn how Brenda darkens the hallway next to her bedroom to create a place to walk, as if she is "in the woods":

> SALLY: But how do you do that—put yourself in a different place—when you're in your hallway?
> BRENDA: Well, because I kind of use my imagination because you see the things [a poster in her hallway with trees] and you pretend it's the trees in the woods and you kind of put yourself in that spot and you kind of think of that, like that.

Brenda satisfies her own requirements for "real" and "fake." It's real for her inside the teepee because it's like being inside a drama. She explained to me that the miniature model of a pueblo she made in Mrs. Lefkowitz's class last year as part of their social studies unit doesn't allow that same surround and, consequently, the same feeling of active exploration. In contrast, with the teepee she makes, she can experiment with lighting to create shadows or darkness and then experience it directly. She can even move a tree she sees outside her window into the space as a prop—from back stage to on stage, by seeing it that way. As she told me, she even scares herself sometimes, but she can turn on the lights and turn them off again; she can reach out and touch the bed and know she is in her very own bedroom.

Similarities and Differences

Brenda says all the indoor activities are fun, but camping emerges as the play Brenda likes best. I have identified three features or characteristics similar for each play type: (1) Each activity calls for two or more players; (2) each uses the space Brenda calls the playroom; and (3) each has control and agency as a theme. Features 1 and 2 need no further explanation, but the theme of control and agency is an interpretation and examples will help to illustrate my thinking.

In hide-and-seek, Brenda takes control as follows: She sometimes manipulates the lights, keeps secret the fact that she can see Catherine behind the curtain, and makes the game more complicated. In playing house, the cousins appear to play more cooperatively (or it could be, to use Brenda's phrase, Catherine "gets her own way" when they play house). What the children "control" when playing house are their roles and the transformation of objects and spaces (e.g., the closet that becomes the elevator; the doll who becomes the neighbor).

In camping out, Brenda takes over much or all of the control. She is the expert here; she is also set designer, script writer, casting director, and producer. The script may change in the future, however, as she makes room for Mandy, who is her same age and her best friend.

There are differences between and among the three activities Brenda plays indoors. Five additional characteristics reveal these differences; they are (1) affiliation; (2) control of the environment; (3) a three-dimensional structure; (4) complexity; and (5) Brenda's phrase "make it real." Unlike hide-and-seek and playing house, what Brenda calls camping—and I call worldmaking—contains all five features and are what makes this play fun for her.

1. *Affiliation.* Affiliation, by which I mean close association and membership, characterizes playing house and camping out but not hide-and-seek, where competition is a compelling feature.

2. *Control of the environment.* Control of the environment is very strong in camping, less so in the two other indoor activities. An example is Brenda's turning off the lights at night. Controlling the light is also a feature of hide-and-seek, but in camping Brenda not only turns off the light but keeps the TV on; sometimes the campers watch it, sometimes its flickering light helps create the spooky feeling Brenda wants to achieve. Additionally, using a bag she has cut to look like flames and colored red, she pretends to build a fire so they can eat marshmallows.

3. *Three-dimensional structure.* Brenda builds the teepee herself. It is an enclosure that simultaneously hides and houses the players. In contrast, when the girls play hide-and-seek and when they play house, they do not build anything.

4. *Complexity.* Brenda brings to camping a script, props, and scenery that are more complex and varied than those used in playing house or hide-and-seek. She not only builds a three-dimensional structure but also creates a world that is true to her experience and worthy of her vision.

5. *"Make it real."* Brenda does not refer to hide-and-seek as incorporating real people, a real world. Playing house and camping are different in that respect, but Brenda says she works to make it seem that way:

> BRENDA: So with the dolls we make it like there's really a neighbor and we're really in a house with the mother working while the child's at school.
>
> SALLY: I see. But how come this is not "pretend"?
>
> BRENDA: Well, we just (*she sighs*) try to make it seem real like we're REALly camping out and we're REALly in our house with the neighbor and everything.

SALLY: So is it more of a matter of the way you think about it rather than—

BRENDA: Right. We use our imaginations to make it real.

The Importance of Being in It

As stated earlier, Brenda draws from three experiences when building and playing inside her teepee; to some extent, each helps her reproduce, replicate, or connect to really camping. First, there is her actual experience with her family—it was apparently brief, but it made a strong impression on her.[4] The problem Brenda must solve is how to reproduce those experiences for herself and her playmates inside a small bedroom—how to replicate the same feelings using two chairs, a sheet, and a paper bag torn and colored red (the fire).

Second, there is that moment in her second-grade classroom when, under the teacher's direction, they put together a large "teepee" made of sticks and brown paper and took turns going inside it. This teepee, however, unlike school library books, cannot be taken out on loan. But Brenda clearly remembers her teacher telling the class of another design possibility—use two chairs and a sheet. She will try it.

Third, there is both the inspiration and practice Brenda may have gained from making a model of a teepee, also an activity in her second-grade classroom. Brenda seems to have enjoyed this experience and describes what she did in detail. However, and she emphasizes this point, making the model of a teepee is not the same for her as being inside a teepee. She explains why using the analogy of making herself small to explore a doll's house.

> Because what I'm trying to say is: it's fun making the real big things so you could BE in it. Because like I said about the doll house, I would like to be in a doll house, and you could go inside and see the things and go up the stairs—see the roof and everything. It'd be fun. That's what I mean: You could both [be in] the real thing and see how it really feels.

---

4. When Monifa read this part, she questioned whether Brenda had actually camped outside overnight with her family or had simply picnicked with them—perhaps somewhere outside the city. On her own, she asked Brenda and is convinced that the family merely went on a picnic. I do not think Brenda misled me; rather I think I assumed she had had to experience camping out to know its essentials. If Monifa is correct, then somehow, without the direct experience, Brenda has been able to assemble the pieces.

With her teepee (see Photo 4.1), she has something big enough to get inside; she does not have to imagine herself small so as to explore what it feels like, it feels like it's for real because she can "BE in it."

Finally, although Brenda borrows the word *teepee* to name her shelter, she does not pretend to be like the Native American people she studied. Nonetheless, for me, Brenda is connected to a long tradition—call them pioneers, explorers, wanderers. On their journeys and explorations, they stop and build a temporary shelter where they refresh themselves before continuing. To build the shelters, they use what they have brought with them, supplemented by materials found nearby. The design of their shelter is a traditional one, handed down from one generation to another but changing with local conditions. A fire is built. The people gather to eat. Soon talk of the day's events move to stories of other times. One by one, children, then adults find room within the small shelter. Noises break the dark stillness and interrupt dreams. A child lifts the tent flap and looks beyond the shadows. She thinks of the promise of morning and, with it, family and friends coming together to begin a new day.

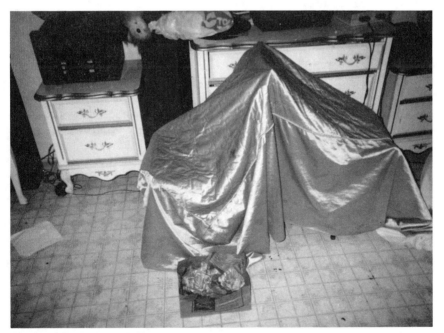

Photo 4.1. Brenda's Teepee

5 ISAAC:
Chit-Chat Behind a Curtain

Isaac brings in 11 photographs taken with the disposable camera I sent home with him; all were taken by his mother. Only one photograph is taken outdoors; Photo 5.1 shows Isaac standing by himself in front of the recently built high-rise apartment building where he lives with his parents and two older brothers. Hair neatly combed, Isaac is dressed in matching nylon warm-up jacket and pants. He is holding a basketball.

In one important respect, this photograph gives a false picture because Isaac plays mostly indoors. He plays inside his apartment because streets, sidewalks, and parks are experienced as unsafe. Isaac's mother, a teacher's aide in his school whom I spoke with often, tells me: "Oh, I never let any of my sons go downstairs by themselves. And, you know, I tell him, you know, sometimes, you know, you're just in the wrong place at the wrong time."

I start this chapter by looking at the "library" Isaac sets up in the living room. Next, we open the bedroom door and enter two invented worlds where Isaac reigns as puppeteer and storyteller. In one, he strategically plans the attack and manipulates the fates of toy soldiers. In the other, hidden by a blanket, he sits on his bunk bed, where he makes funny noises and "chit-chats," his word, with a favorite stuffed toy.

A "LIBRARY" IN THE LIVING ROOM

Isaac sets up a "library" in the family living room. This play is interesting because it shows his making sense of readers' habits—some buy, some take books out on loan—and how few props he needs to create a stage for his play; it is an example of what one child sees as essential in the adult world of work.

Photo 5.1. Isaac Outdoors

Between two chairs Isaac places a board his mother uses as a back support; this is the "desk," he tells me, adding that his mother doesn't let him put books "all around the house." He puts books on a chair and makes a sign. (I neglected to ask what the sign says.) He also makes paper money for those customers who want to buy books they like a lot. "But if you don't like them so much, you could borrow them—you could read them. And if a book's very interesting that you like, you could buy it with the paper money." Isaac's usual customers are his 11-year-old brother, Reuben, and his mother.

ISAAC'S SPACE

Isaac shares a bedroom with his two older brothers (only Rueben is at home now as the 16-year-old is enrolled in a school upstate). This bedroom, because of its limited space, allows for few changes (see Figure 5.1). Isaac says: "I can't change the room around. All I can do is move this bed up to this bed and make it like a big "T." Additionally, there are adult concerns and directives. For example, when I ask Isaac's mother if she would notice his using a blanket or sheet for his play, she is quick to respond: "You're

Figure 5.1. Isaac's Drawing

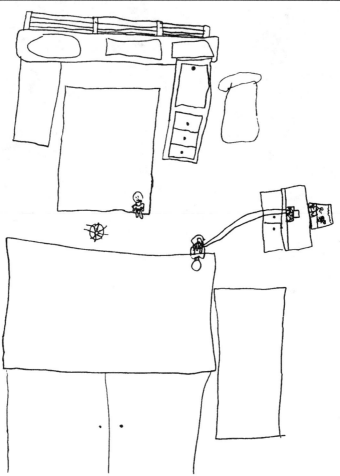

talking to their mother. They're taking my sheets, I would have noticed that! (*She laughs.*)"

Forced sharing of limited space adds this difficulty: an inability to keep special things secret, that is, hidden from others. "There's not so many hiding spots," according to Isaac. He gives as an example his older brother's attempt to hide a board game. But how does Isaac find out? In the passage that follows, he explains how he takes advantage of circumstance and a timely observation.

Because I/because he had tooken it out. So when he said, "Don't look," right? 'Cause our door can't shut 'cause the people who made our door, they didn't make it the exACT size. So/so there's an opening. And I was looking through it, and I saw he had put it in the closet.

The polite but persistent questions Isaac's classmate Rick asks during the initial interview help me understand most, but not all, of what's in Isaac's drawing (see Figure 5.2).

RICK: Excuse me, but what is this? (He points to the feature I have since labeled A.)
ISAAC: This part? (*He points not to A, but to B.*)
RICK: No, this (*he points again to A*).

Figure 5.2. Isaac's Drawing with Selected Features Identified

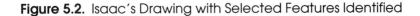

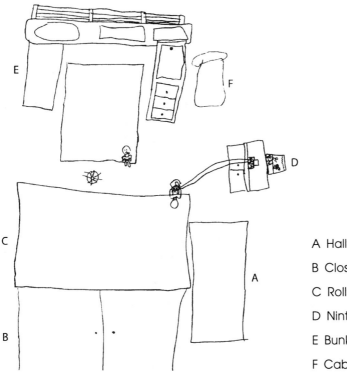

A Hallway door

B Closet

C Rolling bed

D Nintendo and TV

E Bunk Beds

F Cabinet

Isaac: That's the doorway to go out.

Rick: So what is these? (*He points to B.*)

Isaac: The closets. The closets in our room. And this is a rolling bed
[C], so it could move and the closet could open.

Slowly, with Rick's questions and Isaac's responses, I make sense of
other features in the drawing, as follows: the cabinet with TV and Nintendo
is D; the bunk beds are E; and a cabinet holding toys is F. The small figure
on the edge of the rolling bed (C) is Isaac's brother, who is shown playing
a video game (Isaac draws the cables stretching from his brother's hands
to the game apparatus located on the top shelf of the cabinet). Isaac draws
himself sitting at the foot of the lower bunk bed.

Rick does not ask about the circle within a circle in the center of the
drawing. After the boys have returned to their class, I count the curvy lines
that start at points along the rim of the inner circle and radiate outward.
Nine. The circles and "arms" appear spinning in place in the center of the
page.

The bunk beds lend themselves to performing feats of strength and for
wrestling, as Isaac explains:

I like go behind the bed I'm sitting on [shown in Figures 5.1 and
5.2], and I'll pull myself up and hang upside down. And sometimes I
jump down from the top bunk to the floor. Yeah.

I like wrestling 'cause all the time, my brother Reuben, he's able
to do the Razor's Edge on me. He puts you in between his legs and
he lifts you up and he catches you behind your arms and he drops
you on the bed/floor. But he drops me on the bed.

I am unsure whether or not the boys try to keep these and other more
physical activities secret from their parents.

GI JOES

Sometimes Isaac sets up his collection of GI Joes on the table near the
kitchen and plays as his mother cooks dinner; he also plays in his bedroom. The GI Joes in Isaac's collection are about 5 inches tall and made of
plastic. Not only do they carry different weapons, but their clothing is color-
coded (bright greens, reds, blues, yellows) and they have distinctive hair
cuts and boots. And as I learn from Isaac, each has a name:

He has a Mohawk (*as we talk we are looking at a photo Isaac's mother
took of Isaac with his GI Joes*). And he is wearing a red jacket and red

boots . . . The guy right here, with the yellow . . . his name is She-
bang . . . Right here, with the blue on . . . his name is Shockwave.

Isaac's play with his miniature soldiers is full of action; they just don't
stand around shooting their machine guns and bazookas at each other.
He makes them fly, jump, climb, hide, parachute, launch rockets, fight
hand to hand, stage a sneak attack, die, and come back to life. The action
follows a script, as Isaac explains: "They want, one team wants to rule to
the world, and the other just wants the other people to live in peaceful."
Isaac carefully separates the 20 or so figures in his collection into two
groups: good guys and bad guys. Members of each group are well-armed
for killing:

> They got machine guns, rocket launchers, and you know those
> things with the cannon? Drop the bullet in there, then you press
> something and launches out . . . Or they have a tank or they have
> like they have little machine guns or they got a regular gun.

In this next quotation, Isaac explains how the game starts and I learn there
are many ways for GI Joes to die: "I start off with three people dying. One
shoots the other or one gets hit by a rocket launcher or I crush one or
someone might get shot by a bazooka or rolled over by the tank (*he laughs*)."
I ask just who exactly has died—the good guys or the bad? Isaac replies:

> Isaac: The people who want to rule the world died. The group that
> wants to have the people live in peaceful, THEY killed the bad
> guys.
> Sally: Oh, I see. So that's how it starts. Then what happens?
> Isaac: And sometimes I make the bad guys win and sometimes I
> make the good guys win.

The game never ends: New armies take the place of defeated ones and
the dead return.

> Isaac: Never ends. . . . A new army comes. Like they came back
> from the dead. They have to have to be put in the lava and they
> die. They're dead, fried.
> Sally: But some come back from the dead?
> Isaac: Yeah, they're like robots.
> Sally: Oh, of course.

Furniture items become props. Beds, for example, allow certain actions:
"I put some GI Joes in the middle of the bed so they could like jump off."

The other prop in the war stories Isaac directs is a plastic volcano. It came originally with his set of dinosaurs. In our first conversation, he does not mention it; in our second, he talks briefly about using it as a hiding place for his GI Joes. But it is not until our third conversation, when we look together at one of his photographs showing a small, cone-shaped object, that I recognize the circles with wavy arms in his drawing as a miniature volcano. Isaac reiterates how he uses the volcano when playing with his GI Joes: "Sometimes I make like a sneak attack. I put someone underneath the volcano. They come out. They pop out."

Isaac's play with his collection of GI Joes is tidy, without mess. There is killing, but no blood. People die, but no one cries. There is a volcano, but no lava. I ask if he doesn't sometimes cut up paper and pretend it is spewing out of the cone and onto the floor. He doesn't. For me, this would add to the realism, be fun to do, and be a means to change things—if only in a limited way. But can Isaac do such things? I think not. It would be difficult given the ordered space and others' needs. Hence, landscape, actions, plot, even an erupting volcano must be imagined, and the battle between the good forces and the bad must be carried on in Isaac's head.

In his drawing (refer to Figure 5.1), Isaac and the volcano both appear cool and still. Isaac, however, may be planning a sneak attack.

ISAAC'S "LITTLE HOUSE"

In his bedroom Isaac builds what he calls his "little house." He uses the bunk bed as its frame, its drawers as fasteners, and the lower bunk as the interior. He explains how he builds his little house and what he does inside: "I make homes with my bunk beds. I put a blanket in the back, right here. And then [in the] drawers up here, I put a *cocha*, a blanket. So it could cover all of this and make it dark." Isaac often makes his little house alone, sometimes with his older brother, and still less often with select male friends his age who visit after school.

Building the "Little House"

Five of Isaac's 11 photographs show his "little house." Four of those showing the little house are about building it; the fifth shows Isaac and Reuben sitting inside. Two photographs are included to illustrate the building sequence as Isaac shared it with me:

This photograph [see Photo 5.2], right, I'm just starting, right now. I'm starting to make my house/making my house. Right? This is how I start; this is how I start off: I take a blanket, and I go on the

Photo 5.2. Isaac Building His "Little House"

top bunk bed, and I just—wait. And then I bend down; I open the drawer right here (*he points to the drawer at the far end of the top bunk*). Then I put it in. And after that, I go to the next one.

And that's how it looks when it's finished [see Photo 5.3]. My mother wanted to take a picture of it.

Isaac's mother said that, although she had seen her son's little house, taking the photographs was the first time she had watched him build it.

I've never seen him do this—actually see him do this. I've seen the finished product. I've never seen him go up on the top bunk bed and open the drawers to have to make the sheets stay—I never saw that being done. I always thought maybe his older brother would help him. But you know, he did this himself; he came up with these

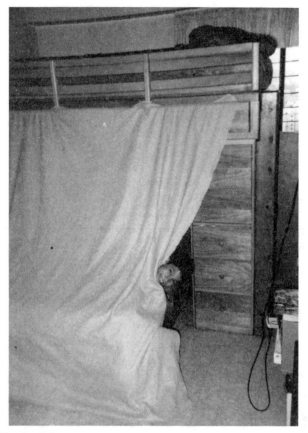

Photo 5.3. Isaac Looking Out from His "Little House"

things himself. So, so interesting seeing him actually tuck the blankets in and just setting up the whole thing and then the things that he does inside.

Isaac reports trying other home designs, but each fails. The problem common to each of these efforts is making the blanket stay in place. He describes one such failure below.

Isaac: It wouldn't stay (*he shakes his head*).
Sally: It wouldn't? So then what did you do?
Isaac: So then I just destroyed it. I just made the regular house.

In the next quotation, Isaac recalls the first time he built his little house.

> ISAAC: I had took a blanket, and I threw on the top bunk bed. And I climbed on the bunk bed. And when I was done/when I got up there/I just put it over. Then that's when I thought putting in the drawers.
>
> SALLY: Oh, and then what did you think after you put it in the drawers?
>
> ISAAC: Then I sort of thought about being a house.

When Friends Come Over

I learn that sometimes Isaac builds his little house when his friends come over. His friends are four boys, aged 8 to 11 years; two are brothers. All the boys live in the same building as Isaac. Wondering how building and playing in his little house gets going when friends are visiting, I ask: "What do you say to your friends?" He answers: "I say, 'You want to make spooky stories?' (*His voice has become quiet.*) So they could come in and they won't be bored."

His friends are not always interested; in those instances, Isaac explains, he does not push his preference. Additionally, to build or not to build the little house when other boys visit appears not to include any suggestion about playing house, playing with doll-like toys, and so forth.[1]

> ISAAC: Some people didn't want to come. So I just left it/I didn't make one. Like sometimes they want to make spooky stories, sometimes they don't. I'll bring in friends and I'll tell 'em stories; or my other friend, he'll tell us spooky stories; or my brother will come in and tell me a very spooky story.
>
> SALLY: Why did you think kids do things like that— make houses like that?
>
> ISAAC: I don't know (*he speaks very softly*). I just do it.
>
> SALLY: Why do you think other kids do it?
>
> ISAAC: So they could do the same thing: make spooky stories or make it is like their little hiding spot or something like that. Make my house and act foolish.

---

1. I am grateful to Mary Rogers for pointing out to me that a possible reason for Isaac's friends not wanting to build and play in his little house was because they considered it girls' play.

Isaac Inside, but Not Alone

In his little house, a blanket on one side and one or more covering the window, Isaac sometimes plays inside with his brother (see Photograph 5.4).

ISAAC: And this is me and my brother trading model cards.
SALLY: So where are you now?
ISAAC: Inside the house.
SALLY: Oh, yeah, inside; now I see the blanket hanging down in the back.

When alone, Isaac listens to his radio and plays with his stuffed animals (a "little bunny rabbit" and two blue bears). He did not mention the stuffed animals in our two previous conversations; it was not until we looked at the photo that shows him trading baseball cards with his brother inside the little house that he confides:

ISAAC: I play with my little bunny rabbit I have. It's all the way back here. See it? (*He points to one of his photographs.*) It's that blue little

Photo 5.4. Isaac and His Brother inside the "Little House"

thing with—and right there, next to it, there's a big trophy. You see it?

SALLY: Yeah.

ISAAC: And you look very closely, there's a little teddy bear. I call 'im "Ted."

The small blue teddy bears and brown rabbit sit on the top shelf in the left section of the bunk beds; these shelves open onto the lower bunk where Isaac sleeps. Because Isaac's drawing shows the bunkbeds from a frontal perspective, I was unaware of any shelves. Partly because he did not talk about them, I did not think to ask. And even though I looked over his photographs before talking with him about them, by concentrating on what the boys were doing, I missed the three stuffed animals on the shelf.

Isaac notices the favored toys in the photograph and confides to me that when behind the blanket, he talks, tells spooky stories, reads books, and plays with his stuffed animals:

ISAAC: I say/I tell spooky stories to myself (*he smiles*) or I talk to myself.

SALLY: Uh huh.

ISAAC: Or I'll beat up my teddies—my bears.

SALLY: Uh huh.

ISAAC: Or read a book in the dark 'cause I have a little night light.[2]

When I wondered how it felt when he was inside, alone, Isaac replies:

Well, I'm actually not; I have my teddy bears. I'll play with them. I make believe they are my friends; or one day they meet each other and they become friends. Or maybe they are friends and they act like a little chit-chat. That's mostly all I'll do.

When I ask if he could tell me more, Isaac is at first silent, then says:

ISAAC: Hmm, for me, it feels all right.

SALLY: Mm hmm.

---

2. Isaac's words "beat up" strike me, and perhaps the reader, as inconsistent, if not disconcerting. These are soft, cuddly toys, and Isaac says he pretends they are his "friends." Because I failed to ask him to elaborate, I am left with my hunch that his play with his toys—like his play with his brother and his male friends—includes wrestling and mock fights. While this may look "aggressive," my sense is that Isaac's "rough-and-tumble play" with either real or imagined friends is not intended to hurt. (To understand better the debate regarding the term *aggressive*, see Block, 1976; Maccoby, 1990; Thorne, 1993.)

ISAAC: For other people, they think, to other people, like to my
mother, she'll yell out: "Isaac, what you doing?" (*He changes his
voice.*) I'll just say, "I'm playing" (*he says this as if he is calling to
someone at a distance*). Or-rr my brother say, "You're crazy."
'Cause I'm talking to myself, playing with my teddy bears that
really don't talk. Unless you have a teddy bear that someone
made up. That teddy bear there used to be [I miss the word he
uses] and his jaw moved and you put a tape in it.

SALLY: Isaac, you're making up this story, right? You don't need any
ole tape that someone else made up—

ISAAC: No.

SALLY: You're doing your own.

ISAAC: Yeah.

SALLY: Yeah. You're like a writer (*I pause*). I think that's not crazy at
all, personally I would call that being creative. I mean, you're
telling the story and you're acting and making them perform.
(*Isaac smiles and nods his head "Yes."*)

6 MICHELLE and AYISHA: Dreamhouse in the Sky

Michelle and Ayisha are best friends. Michelle defines her closeness with Ayisha this way: "I don't go places by myself—I go with Ayisha." As best friends, they have much in common, including the outdoor physical space where they play. In a playground, the girls create a house for a pretend family, and in a tree, they make a clubhouse for friends. I start with these places, then turn to the girls themselves. I follow with more detailed descriptions of playing house indoors and outdoors, exploring the differences. I conclude with their clubhouse, its origins and its end.

THE PLAYGROUND

Ayisha and Michelle are 10 years old and in the same fifth-grade class. They are also neighbors. They live in seven-story buildings opposite each other in a housing project that takes up an entire city block. The spaces in between the buildings are carved up into paved paths, fenced off to protect grass and trees, and blocked out into small playgrounds, each with benches and several pieces of commercial play equipment—this one includes a multilevel metal tower and a smooth cement seal (i.e., the marine animal). Children of all ages climb on them. During the summer, the seal becomes a sprinkler. In all seasons, Michelle and Ayisha remake the tower into a stage for playing house with their friends, cousins, and neighbors.

Asked to draw the places where they play, Michelle and Ayisha drew the small playground between their buildings. In the center of Ayisha's

Figure 6.1. Michelle's Drawing of Playground

drawing and dominating Michelle's is the tower (see Figure 6.1). Michelle shows the tower's levels and the two slides, one curved and the other straight. "Things that people flip on," as Michelle aptly names them, are shown to the lower right of the seal's tail. Michelle draws herself at the right and her cousin, Emet, on the left, standing between benches and the seal's tail. Michelle draws herself jumping rope. She has given herself a broad, curved smile and twinkling eyes. Her upheld arms and the rope complete a circle around her head. She appears to be in her own niche, her arms open to the world.

From the playground, Michelle and Ayisha can walk through an archway on the ground floor of Ayisha's building and emerge onto streets where the traffic of people and vehicles is fast-paced and loud. Growing in the last corner of green in the housing development is the crabapple tree where Michelle and Ayisha say they built their clubhouse. The tree remains; the clubhouse does not. Ayisha made a drawing of their clubhouse (see Figure 6.2).

THE GIRLS

What are the specific strengths that distinguish as well as unite Ayisha and Michelle as friends and worldmakers?

I provide brief impressions of each girl before describing in more detail how they play house—indoors and outdoors—and how, two summers ago,

Figure 6.2. Ayisha's Drawing of Their Clubhouse in a Tree

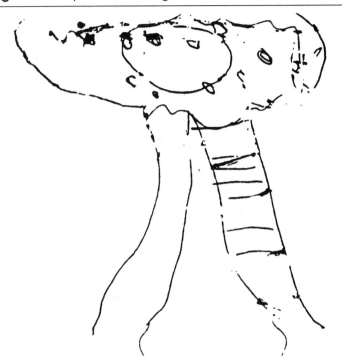

with the help of a boy named Gerard, they built a clubhouse in the "beautiful tree."

Michelle

Michelle is thin and tall, but without brittle edges. There is a softness about her that is apparent when she smiles—which she does often—and in the care she takes with other children. But she is also a fighter and, moreover, she takes her play seriously.

A Caring and Inclusive Child. In her play, Michelle assumes nurturing roles. With her younger cousins, she plays the mother: dressing, bathing, and cooking for them. Outside, she buys them ices and shares her bag of pretzels. She also supervises their play and, by doing so, guarantees that they have opportunities to play outdoors (see Whiting & Edwards, 1988).

When I ask Michelle why it is that so many younger children—in addition to her cousins—want to play with her, she credits the "niceness" of herself and Ayisha:

> 'Cause they like to play house with us. 'Cause like probably they like to play 'cause we nice people. OR, 'cause we treat them nice. Some other people, they be hitting [them]. We don't hit them. We just say, "You do that again, then you not going to play the game." So they say, "All right, I'll be good, I'll be good." We give them one more chance.

Caring and inclusiveness are also qualities of Michelle's relationship with a group that includes girls her own age and slightly older. (In addition to Ayisha, the group includes Mika, 11 years old, and Leontye and Munchkin, both 13 years old.) For example, although the three girlfriends do not help find the wood to build the clubhouse, they are soon included in building it and are then invited inside, as I will explain more fully in the last section.

A Fighter. Michelle wrestles at home with her 16-year-old male cousin, but it isn't this "fighting" I refer to here. Rather, it's her spirited defense of herself, as revealed in the quotation that follows. She provides descriptions of her life at home and of herself as someone who must fight to hold her own. What starts the exchange is my asking why she thinks some adults see kids her age as "not doing anything worthwhile." She replies:

MICHELLE: They probably think we're la-zy.
SALLY: Hmm.
MICHELLE: 'Cause at my house, I am lazy.
SALLY: At your house you are lazy?
MICHELLE: Mm hmm. 'Cause sometime I have to do some work. Then, 'cause everyday, I get money. 'Cause I earn my money by come in the house, do my homework; come from school, do my homework; get my clothes ready for school; go outside; come up at 8:30 and take my shower, eat and watch TV a little bit then get ready for bed. I go to bed at 10 o'clock, that way I can get up early.
SALLY: That doesn't sound so lazy.
MICHELLE: I know. 'Cause sometimes I don't like taking a shower 'cause it be boring. Or, when I have to do something, I get mad. Because I always got to do something—nobody else do nothing. And everybody always picking on me in my house.

A Serious Player. In our second conversation, Michelle shares how she and her girlfriends think about playing house; she says, "For us, it's fun to pretend like we are mothers—to see how it feels. 'Cause when we pretend, we see how it feels."

At the time I was surprised at Michelle's assertion—not that pretending was fun, but that, to her thinking, it was purposeful. In our fourth conversation, I return to her interpretation of why they play and again ask about it. Patiently, she explains.

> MICHELLE: Me and Ayisha, we practicing because, see, we want to know how it feels to have our own house and how it feels to be a mother.
> SALLY: Uh huh. I see. So you are practicing. I thought you said, "We only pretend." (*She shakes her head "No."*) So, does this seem right: By pretending, you are practicing?
> MICHELLE: Yep.

I want to know how she understands "real" and "pretending like." Does she see their relationship differently? I ask: "So how do you make it like real?" This is the first time either of us uses the word *real.*

> MICHELLE: We make it real 'cause we act like we really/we really are a mother and that we really own our own house.
> SALLY: So at the time you're doing it, it seems real? (*Michelle nods her head "Yes."*) When are the times when it doesn't seem real?
> MICHELLE: (*She looks up, shakes her head.*) When it doesn't seem real? Hmm (*she pauses*). But it always seems real.

Michelle says they make it real by acting like they "really are" mothers who "really own" the things that mothers are supposed to own—a house, for example. And that, Michelle says, "always seems real."

Ayisha

Ayisha is energetic and confident as she combines ideas with voice and gestures to tell her story or make her case. In front of the video camera, she was articulate and self-assured. (We were in Mrs. Lefkowitz's room, her class having gone on a field trip.) She seemed to know exactly what "being on camera" was supposed to look like. I mostly watched as she took charge. When I suggested she tape her earlier drawings to the chalkboard as a backdrop for our conversation (one drawing showed the playground, buildings, and surrounding stores and the second, the tree and clubhouse), she began making additions with a magic marker. When she ran out of space on the drawings to put in the basketball courts where they sometimes play volleyball, she picked up chalk and started drawing on the chalkboard. The drawing completed to her satisfaction, she picked up Mrs. Lefkowitz's pointer, stood up, and used it as she talked.

A Worldmaker. In addition to turning the different levels of the climbing tower into what she names bedrooms and carports, Ayisha describes how they re-create their world on the playground into a supermarket, baby-sitter's house, school, preschool, a place for parties, and backyard. Each place is an example of how she and Michelle combine a particular physical space, a few essential props, and their imaginations; the latter acts as a kind of glue—a way to cement it all together. I will first use Ayisha's words to describe the supermarket, next the party place, and end in their backyard.

They set up their "fake supermarket" behind a gate: buyers on one side, sellers on the other. Ayisha explains the purpose of the choice of location as follows: "It has a GATE, that way nobody can take it. And we told them [the customers] that if they climb up the gate, they automatically have to sit down." The supermarket opens when friends "bring down" their "fake counter." For sale are the artificial foods—called "toy stuff" by Ayisha—that often come with young children's kitchen sets.

> And they bring toy stuff—'cause they have the fake kitchen and they have foods that go with the fake kitchen . . . And they have bags and stuff . . . And we have our fake money in our pockets, and we ask how much it costs. And they tell us the prices and then we buy it. We come home. We act like we eating it.

When someone brings down a radio, they may dance in a grassy area and pretend they're at a party. The party gets worked into playing house when Munchkin, playing the role of a teenager, tries to sneak into her bedroom. Ayisha picks up the story at the point of discovery.

> AYISHA: And the fake mother, Mika, she's sitting in her room waitin'. And when Munchkin comes in, sometimes she says, "I made it." And when she turns around, Mika is right there and she gets caught, and she gets punished.
> SALLY: Oh, dear. What does "punishment" mean?
> MICHELLE: Like sometimes she doesn't get to go outside; talk to nobody. She has to be stuck in the room all day long.

According to Ayisha, they pretend that another grassy plot is their backyard. They even pick up the litter so, as Ayisha explains, "it could look like it really our backyard." She continues:

We only have cans and stuff that are easy to pick up. And sometimes there's paper. But Housing [the maintenance personnel assigned to the project], they come everyday. They clean the park, they clean the buildings—everything.

An Entrepreneur. As I learn from both girls, a large part of playing house is "watching" younger children. As "mothers," they may pretend to hire Michelle's cousin, Emet, to baby-sit so they can go out, but it is they who are actually taking care of younger cousins and the younger siblings of their girlfriends. Neither girl complains; Ayisha explains why: "We get to watch babies (*her voice gets softer*), we get to watch kids; we get to act like they're our so-ns (*she draws out the word*)."

However, Ayisha and Michelle are making plans. "Watching" children is to become "baby-sitting" children—likely the same children, but now they'll be paid for it. In the past, for instance, the girls sometimes received money to buy snacks for the children they were "watching." They likely ate the snacks, too, but they had no choice in how to spend the money.

The girls see baby-sitting as requiring a greater degree of planning and organization (e.g., using phones, putting out flyers). So far, they have decided on the top administrators and main worker: "Now we starting to plan for the summer. We planning on making a baby-sitter's club. . . . And Mika is the president, I'm the vice president, Michelle is/Michelle is like the baby-sitter."

Know-How

Early on in my knowing Michelle and Ayisha, I imagined them holding a magic wand: They take turns waving it and playground equipment becomes a house big enough for everyone; a simple motion of a hand and everyone keeps their promises to be good ever after.

A second image also emerges from the above snapshots of Michelle and Ayisha. It's their "know-how." Each in her own way knows how to *negotiate and facilitate the play and the players*; knows how to *take care of herself*; knows how to *do things and make things* with the resources available. And, finally, they each know how to *learn by pretending*, to *learn by doing*.

I celebrate their ability to take up a magic wand. With it, they make things happen; they transform themselves, others, and the world around them. By so doing they push against and enlarge the boundaries of space and time.

Waving a magic wand is the pretend part of play. I also learn from them that play includes experimentation and trying on different roles. Through their actions and interactions they practice what it's like—what it really feels like—to be a responsible, caring person. And by so doing, each becomes that person.

PLAYING HOUSE

Playing house is what Michelle and Ayisha do together most of the time—indoors and outdoors. In the summer, they take their play on the road, so to speak, and playing house moves from inside to outside and then back inside again. It is that movement that I describe first, including how their play is a mix of the real and the pretend and how the girls create new play possibilities in response to different seasons and settings.

Play Indoors, Outdoors, and Back Again

To facilitate playing house indoors, Michelle and Ayisha shift both people and things around. Michelle explains the adaptations, moves, and changes to the environment.

> Oh, when we play house, we change a LOT of things around. We change around the bedroom. We act like we going to make the kids sleep in a different room—if they don't behave. OR we change our room to the kids' room, and they put their stuff in our room, and we put our stuff in their room. OR sometimes they sleep with us, OR we go sleep in their room, and they sleep in our room.

She stops and, touching her hand to her head, asks as if to herself: "And what else?" She then continues, "We change the bathroom around." I ask, "How do you do that?" "We put things different places—like lotion and stuff. And when we play house, my mother, she got these broken beepers, and we put them on. Act like we have a beeper."

Michelle then shifts from describing what objects and spaces they use for their indoor play to what playing house means for her. She fixes what's broken, turns limited space into something "big," and makes them owners of the "whole world." "And we act like we own the whole world and that we got a lot of money and we live in a BIG house."

The girls' indoor play is a seamless blending of the real and the pretend. For example, as Michelle's young cousins eat breakfast, she and Ayisha pretend they are "mothers" and are cooking for their children:

> When we play house, we wake up; we cook breakfast. Then we walk around—act like we going to work. And we have my other cousin, big cousin, a fake baby-sitter. And then my little cousins are our kids—one is hers [Ayisha's] and one is mine. And we get them dressed. No, first we give them a bath, then we get them dressed.

Staying over at each other's home also presents new possibilities. For example, if Ayisha sleeps over at Michelle's apartment, they report additional possibilities for play—and eating. Again, if they have money, they purchase real food:

> And then, if she stay over . . . we play. And then we go like out/out and get some Chinese food, and we take them [younger children] with us or we go to the store to get snacks and something to drink or we go to Mika's and eat there.

Sometimes the girls make these visits into a party, as Michelle explains: "Then we come back home. We play games. Act like we having a party with our snacks. And then we run all over the house playing tag and hide-and-go-seek."

Acting Like "Mothers"

Consistently, whether playing house indoors or outdoors, the girls continue to "act like" they are mothers. While adults might view them as older girls caring for younger children, Ayisha and Michelle give greater import to their role by calling themselves "mothers." That being a "mother" rather than an unpaid baby-sitter is more appealing to the two girls is not in doubt. But there is another reason as well. It is found in a quotation I used earlier, in which Michelle says: We want to know "how it feels to be a mother." Pretending to be mothers makes demands on Michelle and Ayisha; two of these demands—childcare and careers—are discussed next.

Childcare. Finding someone responsible to watch their children is a critical issue for the "mothers." The usual choice is Emet, Michelle's cousin and the only boy who regularly plays with them. Conveniently for these working mothers, the baby-sitter lives close by.

We clean up first. And then we get everything set up. And then we go knock on my cousin's door—that's next to my room. We act like that's his house and my house 'cause I got the keys to my room, and he's got the keys to his room. So we knock on his door. Ask is it okay for him to baby-sit our kids. He say, "Yeah."

The duties of the baby-sitter are listed by Michelle in the passage that follows.

We act like that he got to take our children to their doctor 'cause they sick—they got a cold; he got to take them to school, pick them up, then give them lunch; make sure they take a nap. And if it's a weekend, we go pick 'em up early 'cause we act like that's when we get our check (*she smiles*).

Career. The mothers pay their baby-sitter with "fake Monopoly money." Transactions take place at the "bank." Michelle plays "the bank lady"; Ayisha is a fellow worker; and Emet, using money paid to him for his baby-sitting services, is a customer, making deposits and withdrawals. Michelle explains the procedure: "I act like I'm the bank lady. 'Cause I got this thing that where you put money—pennies and cards. But you got to wait on line."

Where does Emet stand in line to make his deposits? What can be the intercom system? Where is the money kept? To solve these problems, the children use spaces and things within the house that look like or function like spaces and things in a bank. What follows is Michelle's description of how they set up their bank in a narrow space between the kitchen and the living room, where, I believe, there is a "counter" of some kind. They use objects from her apartment that, for them, approximate the "real" thing.

Well, I have like a small cup, it's white, it's like a coffee cup; but I put my pens and pencils in there. And then I have my papers on that side; and I have my pads and stuff like that. Then I have the big thing in front of me. It's this/it's a black thing, and it's open, and you put the things in—it's like a lock—and you put it in, take it out, and lift it up. [There's] a side where you put pen-nies; a side where you could put your money [bills]. Then there's another side where you could put paper clips and stuff on the other side.

And then we keep their number—like where we put the cards— and how much money we put/how much money they want . . . And when they bring us the money . . . And we lock it and we hide it some where in my house.

I learn where some of Michelle's ideas for the bank come from as well as some of her props when I ask her if, as a bank lady, she must record transactions. She responds: "Hmm, we write it on paper 'cause when I went to my mother's job."

Visiting her "mother's job" on a "Take Your Daughter to Work Day," Michelle saw what offices and desktops look like; she took incoming messages and communicated with someone who works in another office.

> She [her mother's friend at work] gave me pads and pens and things that you write down messages. And while she wasn't there, she let us take messages for her. And she let us play on her computer. And then I called my friend upstairs—she was at her aunt's office—I was at my mother's desk and to come down. And we went to lunch at McDonald's.

For her helpfulness, Michelle was given "pads, pens, and stuff." She takes all this home with her—pads, pens, images, and experiences—and works them into her play.

BUILDING A WORLD ON A PLAYGROUND

Moving from indoors to outdoors opens up new possibilities for playing house as well as new problems that must be resolved. The girls' drawings and the photographs I took of them on the playground provide two sources for understanding how the girls turn the large, multilevel climbing tower into their "fake house," the playground space into a community, and other children into fellow worldmakers. In the discussion that follows, I begin with Michelle's drawing of the playground and follow with the photograph I took showing almost the same view.

The Tower That Becomes Their House

As I said before, taking center stage in Michelle's drawing—as it does in her outdoor play—is a large climbing tower (refer to Figure 6.1). In her frontal view of it, there are three basic parts: a central tower, a slide, and a ladder.

Michelle divides the tower into three rectangular compartments. Each is on a different level and therefore similar to floors in a building or multi-story house. The compartments are between two poles that are rounded at their tops and banded in three places. Michelle draws these bands as parallel lines, slightly curved. By so doing, she adroitly creates a sense of roundness (the effect works best on the left pole). Attached to the pole on the right side of the tower is a slide with handrails at its top. The straight, parallel lines Michelle uses to create this feature narrow gradually so that, like a slide, it truly seems to pick up speed as it leaves the page. The feature attached to the pole on the left loops around to make a giant C. Seventeen parallel lines divide the C, giving it the appearance of a ladder with steps.

As Michelle draws it, the uppermost level does not come to the top of the poles. This level is designated the top floor when they play house. Above it, Michelle draws a peaked roof (the original drawing shows two attempts to make a roof before the final one). As with the slide, the seal, and Emet's hand, a piece of the roof is off the page. In this case, the peak of the roof is not shown. "Sometimes we put a roof on top," explains Ayisha, and Michelle continues with an example: "Yeah, 'cause we have blankets that extra and we just like try to make it. And one long stick that we put under it—to hold it up. That way it could look like a roof." As the girls talk, they draw yet another picture of the climbing tower. Ayisha does most of the drawing and the talking. Like Michelle's version, this "house" also has a roof; but added to it is a chimney and a puff of smoke (see Figure 6.3).

I meet separately with Michelle and Ayisha a month later. At these meetings, Michelle tells me: "We act like it's a roof up there (*she pauses*) with a chimney," and Ayisha provides a helpful distinction between their imagining something (*a chimney, for example*) and it's actually being there. Both ways work for her, as she explains: "Sometimes . . . we do with our imagination, and sometimes we do it."

Documenting Their Play with Photographs

In the middle of my first conversation with Michelle and Ayisha, excited by what they are telling me about themselves and what they do and play, I blurt out my doubts:

> SALLY: How am I ever going to find out about this? I mean, you do it, but I'm a stranger.
> AYISHA: Probably you come over and be with us—
> SALLY: Could I do that?
> (Ayisha and Michelle shake their heads vigorously, "Yes.")

Eager to take Michelle and Ayisha up on their invitation, I plan to meet them after school the next day to take photographs of them at play. Ayisha says she will ask her aunt; Michelle, her grandmother.

Figure 6.3. Ayisha's Drawing of Their Pretend House in the Playground

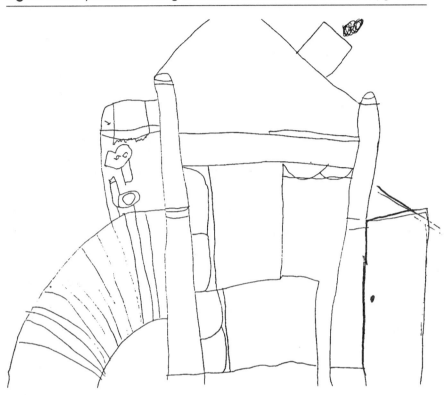

Fortunately, if unexpectedly, the other girls they play with also appear in the playground the afternoon of our meeting and so are included in the photographs. (Emet, however, arrives too late for the playground shots but does appear in the photographs showing the tree where the clubhouse was built.) After a group shot sitting on a bench with their science teacher (I had asked Monifa to accompany me), the girls start to play and I take their picture.

It's likely that both Michelle and Ayisha would have taken different pictures and from different angles than I do, but their perspectives are not entirely lost. Later, when they talk about the photographs, their descriptions are vivid and immediate—it's as if, seeing themselves "there," they can recapture the talk, the actions, the sense of it. For example, when I ask Ayisha why she chooses particular photographs to talk about, she responds: "Because some of these photographs tell the stories, like I was showing you in my pictures [drawings]." Finally, as the following quotations show, although the two of them talk with me separately about photographs I took, they pretty much agree on the basic script of their play. The description that follows is from my conversation with Michelle.

> Well, this is the picture where we play house at. You see where is me, Munchkin, Leontye, and Mika. We always playing house. And we telling the little boy Anthony/we was telling him/we act like we tell him to get ready for school: "Go wash up." And it's time to wake up.
>   This is the picture [see Photograph 6.1] when we just woke up. And we're playing/we're planning on getting up, and we going to ask our mothers for, we have some money like for when we get lunch and stuff.

"Pretend" Worlds Have "Real" Problems

I turn now to how the girls remake what's available in the playground into material for their worldmaking and then discuss how roles are filled. I begin with the young children who are eager to play, then discuss the roles the girls take on, and conclude with their experiences and views of involving boys in playing house.

Remaking What's There. I earlier cited the girls' remarks concerning their ability, when they have to, to imagine a roof and a chimney above their heads. In the quotation that follows, Michelle speaks of how they use the ladder of the tower as "steps" to a door and particular bolts on the metal bars as the "door knob." (Her reference is to an enlarged photocopy I had made of Photograph 6.1.)

> MICHELLE: Those are the STEPS . . . you just come up the steps, knock on the door, and then they let you in.
> SALLY: Okay, there is no door, but do people pretend like there's a door and they go like, "knock, knock"?
> MICHELLE: They knock like on here (*she points to one of the metal crossbars*).
> SALLY: Oh, they actually make a sound?
> MICHELLE: Yeah.
> SALLY: So they knock first, and then walk up the steps?
> MICHELLE: They knock and then (*she smiles*) we act like we open the door 'cause there's little knobs on there which you can't see [on the photograph we are looking at]—but there's little knobs. We

Photo 6.1. Children in the Playground

act like we twist them (*she makes a twisting motion with her right
hand*) and we act like we open the door.
SALLY: Of course.

In this way, Michelle and Ayisha opportunistically use what's already
there, permanent and fixed in place. Here are two other examples. They
use the concrete seal statue as their car. However, if bikes are available,
they make them into their cars. In either case, they use what they have.
"We act like the seal, our car. Or, if somebody like my cousin, he bring
out his bike . . . we act like our car, and we ride around the park, telling
'em we going shopping."

Other Children. Although the repertory company stays pretty much the
same (the regulars consist of Michelle, Ayisha, three girlfriends, Michelle's
younger female cousins, and her male cousin Emet), Michelle reports that
a group of "extras" (younger children) is always hoping for parts when
the girls play house on the playground. She says: "Every time I come outside, they say: 'You going to play house?' We say, 'No, not today . . . we
play tomorrow.'"

I noticed this phenomenon while taking photographs of Michelle and Ayisha in the playground. As they sat with their three friends on the lowest level of the tower enjoying a handclapping game, a younger boy and girl stood watching nearby and another boy watched while hanging upside down from the second level of the tower.

Playing outside as opposed to playing inside an apartment allows more children to be involved. Almost 5,000 people, the majority of them children, live in the housing development where Michelle and Ayisha are growing up. The playground where they play is one of five in the housing development. Thus, how to facilitate and negotiate the large numbers of children who want to play with them is part of playing the game. Michelle explains:

> We tell them we were there first. Then we tell 'em, "Excuse us, don't step on everything because you might step on somebody's ha-nd, or somebody's arm, or somebody's foot; or step something that belongs to somebody." 'Cause they like to run around or slide. So they go there . . . or they go to the benches and talk or play or they go to that other park.

On the other hand, as Ayisha explains next, when the "regular people" are not available, they need other players: "We just use the regular people all the time. [But] if that person can't come outside, we ask somebody, 'You want to play?'"

Girls' Roles. Michelle, Ayisha, and their three girlfriends play traditional women's roles: mother, daughter, and sister. Since 13-year-old Mika always plays the "fake mother," as Michelle and Ayisha consistently refer to her, that causes the remaining girls to act as her teenage daughters, who may or may not be young mothers themselves. The younger children who clamor to play with them then become their children.

Ayisha and I talked about roles and relationships among the players. I include what she told me as representative of both girls' play. For example, Ayisha adds this information about how roles are decided and by whom:

> All right, when we decide, we ask. All right, we already know that Mika is going to be the mother—and we don't have to worry about that. And I'm going to be the sister. The only thing that, Michelle got to decide what she going to be; Leontye Colon, and the other Leontye has to decide what they going to be.

Ayisha next explains that whether players will be cast as "friends" or "family" depends on the number of people available: if just a few, the girls play relatives; if many, they can choose to be a friend:

> Sometimes we don't want them to be friends 'cause they're just little, little people. But if they want/but if there's a LOT of people, we'll let her be a friend . . . But when there's a little people, she'll be like a relative or something, a relative.

A "relative" is usually a sister. First I ask the age of the sister and then their mother's age.

AYISHA: I'm like 21 or 19, 17, 18, or 19.
SALLY: Okay, how old is your mother? How old is Mika?
AYISHA: Umm. We/we don't really/we don't really get into that. But, she's a age when she's not old, old, old, old.

Boys' Roles. As for the boys, the younger ones who want to play are assigned the parts of "sons" and "brothers." But where are the boys their own age?

From Michelle I learn that few boys her age play with them and when they do, they play scary parts where the action pivots around a chase: monster chasing girls and children, robber being chased by children and girls. In each scenario, the villain is a bad man and the women and children, at some point, are in danger. In contrast, cast as the baby-sitter, Emet plays a helpful role. Nonetheless, like the monster and the robber, he remains an outsider—not a member of the family.

When neither Michelle nor Ayisha mentions playing much with boys their age, I ask Michelle if a boy sometimes play the "father" of the family. She shakes her head. "Never," she says. When I later ask Ayisha the same question, she says, "We act like he/he doesn't exist."

I then ask Ayisha to tell me about any times when boys played with them. She recounts one memorable experience: a time when three brothers (triplets) took on the parts of uncle, godfather, and father.

AYISHA: Yes, it was REAL fun 'cause it lasted—the game—from morning, from like afternoon, from after school, until like the time we had to go up like at eight or 8:30 . . . And it was FUN.
SALLY: Tell me about the fathers and uncles—who were they?
AYISHA: Um, the triple, one the triple is/will be the father, one of them be the godfather, the other one be the uncle.

SALLY: I wonder what made them play?

AYISHA: Probably 'cause sometimes we go to after-school program, and they close early. And when they come out/when they come out the program, there's nothing for them to do. There's/they have to go in and look at TV and look at tapes and listen to music and stuff.

SALLY: So these were boys you already knew?

AYISHA: Hm hmm.

SALLY: You've never been able to get them back into a game like that?

AYISHA: Never.

I follow with a question that asks Ayisha to reveal her play preferences; namely, does she want boys her age and older to play with them? She begins by saying she does; however, mid-sentence, she explains how boys' play doesn't fit with girls' play. When boys pretend, she says, they act like they are fighting; but their "play fightin'" gets out of hand and that's scary. Ayisha's response is a concise summary of her thoughts regarding major differences between boys' and girls' play: "Yes, once in a while, but not all the—. And sometimes they get a little too out of hand—they like fighting, they like play fightin'. (*She pauses.*) They start going cra-zy."

A CLUBHOUSE IN A TREE

In this section, Michelle and Ayisha describe the clubhouse (others might call it a treehouse) they built two summers ago with their girlfriends and a neighbor—a boy named Gerard. There are several differences between the clubhouse and their outdoor play house. For example, neither Michelle nor Ayisha refers to what they do in the clubhouse as "playing house" and they do not call it a "fake house." Whereas the fake house is imagined within the multilevels of a metal climbing tower in a playground, the clubhouse is built among the branches of a crabapple tree that grows on the edge of the housing project (see Photograph 6.2). Although the flow of people is heavy in both locations, the tree provides a degree of invisibility. But not quite enough. Whereas playing house goes on outdoors in the playground day after day, their clubhouse experience is brief.

Building

How did their clubhouse begin? Who built it and how? Where was the clubhouse located?

Photo 6.2. The Street Corner Where the Clubhouse Was Built

Their Creation Story. One day two summers ago, when Michelle and Ayisha were out roller-skating, they met their neighbor Gerard, who told them he had found some wood. He suggested they use the wood to build a clubhouse. After a brief discussion, they agreed and helped him find more wood. The girls went to Michelle's house to get their sneakers and rejoined Gerard. After he fashioned a hammer, building began. And now in Michelle's words:

> See, Gerard, he was walking around, and we was skating. And then he said, "Look what I found, some wood!" I said, "What we going to do with wood?" He said, "Make a clubhouse." I said, "So then we going to make a clubhouse out of wood?" (*She says sarcastically.*) He said, "Sure."
>
> So then I went upstairs, put on my sneakers, and Ayisha went upstairs and put on her sneakers 'cause she stayed over my house that day. And so he got something (*she pauses*); he made something like a hammer. 'Cause he had string, he had a stick—a stick and some string . . . He found a small brick put it on the thing, and he taped it around.

Gerard is the same age as Michelle and Ayisha and lives in Ayisha's building, but he does not attend the same school. He is mentioned only in connection to building the clubhouse. However, making the clubhouse was not a solo operation. Gerard has the idea, but the girls help him find more wood; Gerard makes a hammer and then uses it to nail the wood in place, but Michelle and Ayisha pass wood and nails up to him as needed. Michelle recalls: "Gerard, he be up there; and I be at the bottom, passing the stuff."

Location and Selection. I ask both girls about the site selection process. Michelle recalls the discussion among the three of them and their coming to an agreement. Ayisha says their decision was arbitrary to a large extent, but they did test the strength of the tree's branches and, besides, they wanted their clubhouse to be close to home. Michelle recalls:

> MICHELLE: I said, "That's a nice tree." Ayisha said, "It is." And Gerard said, "Well, let's build the clubhouse." I said, "So come on."
> AYISHA: We just choosed it. And we found out how strong it was. And how it was when we stepped on it. You know, like if you was to step on any other branch, that it would bounce, and these didn't. So we thought that was the strongest one.
> SALLY: Now why this particular tree?
> AYISHA: You don't have to walk far just to go to your house—it's right around the neighborhood . . . We didn't want it to be like all way on 106 when we live on 109 [I've changed the streets but kept the distance she uses].

With an enlargement of the previous photograph in front of her, Michelle points out the location of their clubhouse in the crabapple tree. According to her, first Gerard made the bottom, then the sides, and last, the roof. When I ask how they managed to keep the wood in place, Michelle uses an analogy: the bottom and the sides of the clubhouse are like her standing between two people, pushing hard with her elbows against each person: "We had it [wood] close, real close to it [branches] . . . We had close like that, real close. And it didn't fall . . . So it holds you real tight (*she crosses her arms in front of her*)."

Michelle also describes the clubhouse roof, window, and the door that didn't fit. To make their roof, they nail wood along the sides. Because they slant inward, there's no more to do; the sides make do for the roof. She says: "We nailed it well on top; we nailed it on the sides. Then it went up like that and so we just left it like that." Regarding the window, Michelle says a sheet covering a hole allowed easy access as well as a way to cool the interior: "We made/we made something like a window—or a hole. 'Cause we have something like a small sheet. We could get in and out. Or when it's hot, leave/we leave it open."

They want a door but have difficulty finding something that fits—that's not too wide, for example. One thing they try is "thick," says Michelle, and they are unable to make it "smaller." I neglected to ask if they found another door. Michelle talks later in this same conversation about having keys to the clubhouse.

"Helpers." Their three girlfriends do not help find wood for the clubhouse, but they do show up in time to help pass the wood already found up to Gerard. Moreover, according to Michelle, Mika supplies the paint they will use to decorate their clubhouse: "See, but it wasn't that hard because we had some helpers. And/and my friend, Mika, "fake mother," she had paint in her house, so we painted it."

Hearts, Stars, and a Nest

After the paint dries, they all write their names on the outside of the clubhouse and then add embellishments.

> MICHELLE: The next day it dried. We put decorations on it, and we did our names.
> SALLY: Oh. That was on the outside or the inside?
> MICHELLE: The outside.
> SALLY: Uh huh. Whose names?
> MICHELLE: Mika. It was Michelle, Ayisha, Gerard, Mika, Munchkin, Leontye, and Leontye, then my little cousins (*she pauses*), Emet.
> SALLY: What kinds of decorations?
> MICHELLE: We put hearts, stars (*she pauses*). And that's it.

On top of the clubhouse, Michelle adds, they put "a little nest so birds can come and fly on top." I am genuinely surprised by this whimsical addition. But then, Michelle's play, as I remarked on earlier, is caring and inclusive. For example, the bedrooms in the fake house are divided until they can accommodate even the largest family. Similarly, by adding the nest to the top of their clubhouse, Michelle makes room for, extends refuge to, another creature.

However, unlike the fake house on the playground where all are welcome—as long as they behave—Michelle and Ayisha open the clubhouse only to Michelle's cousins and their closest friends. Perhaps that's the reason they never refer to it as a playhouse or "fake house."

Inside the Clubhouse

The occupants of the new clubhouse bring things from home and other things they make as decoration. Ayisha says they brought her grandmother's radio to the clubhouse; on Michelle's list is a radio and, in addition, a "small TV" and a "little fan." Of the three items brought from home to the clubhouse, two provide entertainment and one, comfort. Michelle says they also brought things they made at the summer recreational program they attended. These things are not functional, but decorative: "We go to the Center, and we make things, and we take 'em and put them in the clubhouse. Sometimes for decoration. To make it look pretty."

Unlike some children who form clubs, Michelle and Ayisha do not have a password or identification card to gain entrance; however, they do have three rules. Moreover, only Michelle, Ayisha, and Gerard have keys. Keys and rules go together, as Michelle makes clear: "We got to make sure that we always lock it . . . and like, in the morning, we go check on it."

When I ask Michelle how the other girls feel about not having keys, she tells me instead how she goes about inviting them to play: "'Cause, sometimes in the morning, I go pick up Mika and Munchkin, and they come in the clubhouse." Michelle lists their rules as follows:

> We can't invite other people in (*she pauses*) our house that we don't know . . . The second rule was they had to give permission from one of us. And the third rule was, unless they don't get permission, they um, we got to go pick them up, and then they come with us, and we always got to stay together.

Why Build?

When I ask Michelle why children might build a clubhouse, she answers both for other children and for herself.

> MICHELLE: Some of the reasons they built/we built the clubhouse/ some of the reasons they build the clubhouse because (*she pauses*) sometime it be boring and you want to be alone. Or sometimes when you get yelled at—you don't feel like being embarrassed— so you be in the clubhouse and be by yourself.
> SALLY: Hmm.

MICHELLE: Or, when somebody's bothering you, you go somewhere
else and you be all alone.

When things are boring, says Michelle, a clubhouse is the place to play.
Because it's located "somewhere else," it's a place to escape to. A clubhouse offers sanctuary: a place where you can be alone; where you can
hide out in order to protect yourself, recover yourself.

Following her lead, Ayisha and I talk little about the construction and
decoration of the clubhouse or about any rules instituted following its
completion. Instead, Ayisha tells me about her "dream." In her dream, the
tree and her apartment are connected by what she sometimes describes as
a "ladder," "stairs," or "bridge." (Ayisha can see the tree from her apartment
window and Michelle speaks of calling from the tree to her to come down
and play.) In addition, she describes how, with a bucket tied to a string, she
can order food items from stores across the street from the housing project.
Furthermore, in her dream their clubhouse has a balcony and inside, a full
range of machinery for entertainment and food preparation.

When I dream, I thought that a ladder or a stairs or, you know, one
of those things, that movie—if you ever saw *The Land of the Lost*. It's
like made/it looks like a canoe and it's made of the wood, but it goes
re-al long.

And I thought/I had a dream that it would go all the way to
there [from the tree to her apartment]. And I was thinking that any
time we was hungry all we had to do was walk up the ladder and go
into the house and we ask my grandmother, aunt or uncle 'cause
they pass it, and we could come right back down, and we go back
into the clubhouse.

But the clubhouse . . . has electricity in it. Have a TV and a VCR,
CD player, a cassette player, and a microwave, stove, and everything
. . . And then on the other side—this is the front right here. Then
the other side of the clubhouse, it had like a balcony—a little
balcony—that if you didn't want to go outside, you could just sit
right there.

And if it was too too hot, you just sit right there and have a piece
of your bathing suit and your pants on. You could drink anything
that you want to drink.

And when you wanted somebody to go to the store, there was a
string where the bucket . . . and it had a note in it and some money
in it, and it said: "Send me so and such and so." And I gave him
money and he put the change. And put what I wanted and he sends
it right back up.

Though dependent on others for food and drink, Ayisha never doubts that she has her connections in place: in her design, the lifelines are two ladders, one connecting her to resources provided by her family, the other, to those provided from within the community (see Figure 6.4). Thus situated and well-supplied, she can be at ease ("sitting pretty" comes to mind). And if she pleases, she can view the world from a distance—or as she dreams it, from a "little balcony."

EULOGY FOR A PARADISE LOST

The girls report that relatives and passersby liked their clubhouse and praised their achievement. Each girl shared an instance of adult assessment of their clubhouse. Michelle recalls: "People was looking at us, and they said, 'That's nice what ya'll did; that ya'll made that.'" And Ayisha reports: "And my aunt, she said it looks nice. She had took a picture of it, but she had lost it."

Michelle and Ayisha no longer have a clubhouse. They attempted to keep it out of harm's reach by putting it high in the tree: "'Cause," as Ayisha explains, "people like to come hit it—they like to mess with it. So then we put it up there—we put it higher." Despite their efforts at concealment, "Housing took it down," Michelle tells me, referring to the project's maintenance workers.

Figure 6.4. Ayisha's Drawing Showing Their Clubhouse in the Tree

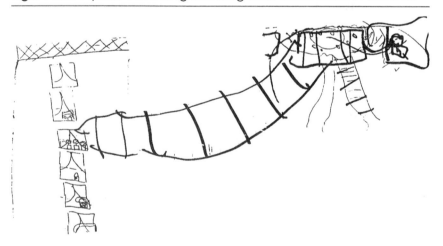

Accompanied by their girlfriends, Ayisha and Michelle led Monifa and me to the site of their clubhouse—the crabapple tree. Once there, the girls climbed the tree and I took photographs. Looking at these photographs a week later, Michelle pinpoints the location of the clubhouse according to where children have placed themselves among its branches. She then shares what she still feels.

And (*pause*) tree had a lot of leaves and stuff and sometime it grow green apples. We was happy with the tree . . . And you can see Ayisha up there. She happy with the tree; Mika happy with the tree; and ALL of us happy with the tree.

Advice to Future Worldmakers

I ask both Michelle and Ayisha what advice they have for other children trying to build clubhouses. Ayisha takes an open approach, one that expresses her confidence both in the cause and in her power to persuade. In contrast, Michelle's advice is to build a clubhouse somewhere where Housing or others in authority cannot find and remove it: "Build it where they could/where they can't find it at, or where they can't take it down . . . go downstairs early [to check on it]. Make sure they don't touch it."

Ayisha advises children to present their case directly to those in authority. In the quotation that follows—perhaps because I am filming as she talks—she acts as if she were talking directly to future clubhouse-builders-of-America. She first reminds them to be careful. She then lays out three arguments to use: Say it's your dream, add quickly that it'll only be there a week, and conclude by emphasizing that you will not blame *them* should there be any accidents.

AYISHA: So, when you make your clubhouse, make sure that it is like nice and built 'cause when you go in it, I don't want none of yous to get hurt—none of yous. I know, I saw some movie, it's called um/this kid made this clubhouse perfect. But the first time he made it, he had fell and broke his arm.

SALLY: Eiyee.

AYISHA: I'm going to give you some advice. Before you make your clubhouse, make sure to tell Housing to leave it up there.

SALLY (*I try to sound unconvinced*): How are you going to convince Housing?

AYISHA: Convince them that it's your dream. And tell them that you wanted to leave it just there for one week. And anything happens to it, that you'll be responsible and everything. And if anything happens to any of us, we would not blame it on you, we would blame it on ourselves. 'Cause we're the one who want to keep it up there. And just go like that.

Building a Dream House

"Housing" represents a basic issue for Michelle, Ayisha, and other children. Namely, to have "somewhere else" for yourself, that place must be where others can't find it; for if they do, they will likely "touch it, take it." In this, however, children have little power. Nor can Michelle and Ayisha wave the imaginary magic wand I put in their hands and, by wishing, cause the clubhouse to reappear. Making a place like a clubhouse in a tree is a complex enterprise: in part, serendipitous; in part, know-how; in part, idea and dream. I will explain.

Someone—usually an adult—must throw away wood or other quantities of suitable materials. Next, kids have to find the materials before they are either hauled off to the dump or hidden inside dark green bags. Should materials be found, then a kid must have the idea and convince others to believe in it. A good site must be found and the building materials transported to it. Tools and additional supplies must be gathered together. What's unavailable must be improvised, and design and structural problems must be solved. Furthermore, it's likely that a team of builders must be assembled and work cooperatively.

With this in mind, it's no wonder Michelle, Ayisha, and their friends sign their names on their clubhouse for all to see, and add hearts and stars. In so doing, they declare their ownership and craftsmanship, their friendship, and their hopes and dreams.

7 MICHAEL:
Stories, Sets, and Action

This is me-e-e. That's my little brother [the smallest figure in his drawing]. I made him small (*he laughs*). These are me [two tall figures, unequal in height, on each side of his drawing]. It's hard to make them the same size . . . I make them as me since/like I do most of the work.

With his drawing between us (see Figure 7.1), Michael explains that the four figures represent himself and his younger brother, Allen. He has drawn his brother and himself in duplicate—one grouping on the left, one on the right—and in each pair, he is the taller, more important figure. But what is the "work" he refers to?

The "work" shown in the drawing is building. "We play like two different games," says Michael. With pillows and bedcover, he carefully builds a casino and a bakery (the structures look alike, but the play is kept distinct); the games the boys play inside their apartment are gambling and cops and robbers.

Michael is one of the tallest boys in his fifth-grade class; like many of his male classmates, he wears the insignia of his favorite basketball team on his T-shirt and cap. Michael, 11 years old at the time of our first meeting in June, and his 9-year-old brother live with their parents in a five-story building on a busy street. On the other side of the street is a municipal park with baseball fields, basketball courts, and an outdoor swimming pool. The park is popular with many neighborhood children and youth but is off-limits for Michael, who is described as "sheltered" by his teacher. It's a short walk for Michael and his brother to and from school, with no major intersections to cross. Their usual route takes them past a *bodega* (Spanish for "grocery store") and a store selling live chickens; at this point

Figure 7.1. Michael's Drawing

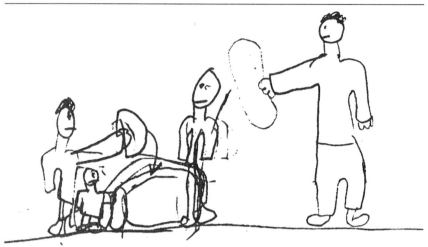

they cut through the housing project where Brenda, Ayisha, and Michelle live.

I begin by introducing the storyteller, Michael, and the stories the brothers act out. I follow their stories with the sets the boys create, including their origins and the structural problems Michael faces each time he builds with pillows. Photographs Michael took show the casino and bakery from several angles as well as the sequence in which he builds them. Then I turn to the action of the boys' play, comparing and contrasting casino and cops and robbers in terms of the structures built, their location, the props used, and the important events in each plot.

But what degree and kind of "action" are possible in a small bedroom with four pillows, one blanket, and two kids? How can this play work for Michael? In the final section, I look again at the game of cops and robbers. Specifically, I consider how the boys rewrite the script, "go on location," switch parts, and dim the lights as ways to sustain their play and keep it fun.

THE STORYTELLER

Basically, what Michael told me is that he and his brother play two games inside their apartment: casino and cops and robbers. Integral to each game is a structure Michael builds with three to four pillows and a bedcover. In casino, the structure stays the same, but in cops and robbers, the bakery that is robbed becomes a police station, a courthouse, and, finally, a jail—then back to a store when the inmate, having served his term, is released.

In my conversations with Michael I was an appreciative audience of one, responding with laughter, comments, and questions both to *what* he had to say and *how* he said it. For example, in response to my question about cops and robbers, Michael asks himself—"And what else do we do?" After an appropriate pause, he provides more information. In this instance, the details focus on characters and plot:

> MICHAEL: Sometimes we like play like if somebody is going to rob the place. Like if some old lady [store owner] lives there. And he [the robber] comes like, "Give me all your money."
> SALLY: And then what happens?
> MICHAEL: I make like a cop. And then I just catch him. And I make like a little house like the jail. So that's what we mostly do.

Michael's questions to himself keep the conversation moving and give it direction; in addition, by asking them, he brings in aspects of his play he judges relevant. Noticeable in the transcripts of our first conversation is that I quickly begin to take my cues from him. For instance, in the quotation above, I ask: "And then . . . ?" I have caught on to his temporal, causal way of storytelling.

In addition to asking himself questions, Michael often supplies dialogue. As he reports past events, he changes his voice and makes exaggerated facial expressions and gestures. In the next quotation, for example, he integrates three pieces of dialogue from the script of cops and robbers; as he does, he accents important words—in this instance, "action," as I try to show by capitalizing it:

> And then when I/I say okay, "ACTION!" Then I run after him like, "You're busted." Then I make the police station/the jail cell. Put him in jail . . . Then the judge says, "You're in this time for 20 years."

Sentencing the robber to jail ends each round of cops and robbers the way Michael and his brother play it. I will describe later the variations they have invented to keep the game going, but for now I want to consider the three voices in the above quotation. First, the voice that says, "You're busted" seems easy enough to identify: It is said to the robber by Michael in his role as policeman. "You're in this time for 20 years" is the sentence handed down by the judge. However, as I learn over the course of four conversations, neither of the boys actually plays the part of the judge. The verdict is heard as if it comes from a voice "on high" or offstage. Spoken with authority, the voice makes it "official"—the robber is guilty and must go to jail.

The boys are not much interested in playing out the trial scene. Michael attributes its speediness to the indisputable quality of the evidence.

SALLY: Does someone play the judge, too, or—
MICHAEL: We just like, like "Judge, I found this guy . . ." We play it different—we don't have a tri-al. We just [say], "Judge, this guy robbed a—" And we just say, "He's in for 50 years?" "Okay, whatever." You know, 15 or 50 or 70, whatever, and just put him in.

Lawyers are absent from the trial scene. I assume their presence would delay the proceedings. It's the roles of cop and robber that the boys take turns acting out; the bakery owner and judge are secondary, and lawyers are not present at all.

Michael plays two parts when he says the word "ACTION!" He is the policeman who tells himself to catch the robber, and he is the director who gives the appropriate cue to start the performance. In this production, Michael both directs and stars. And as we will see, he is also stage manager and set designer.

THE SETS

No matter the game—casino or cops and robbers—the materials (pillows and bedcover) and prop (Monopoly money) are the same; moreover, the structures Michael builds for each game look alike. The difference is in the name given to the setting and the context the boys bring to each.

As I explain next, what the boys build on Sundays when alone at home and bored begins their play. I examine these structures in these three ways: (1) the model Michael builds for me with materials at hand—textbooks and a large plastic trash bag; (2) his photographs; and (3) my schematic drawings. I conclude with a chart that compares playing cops and robbers to playing casino—by location, materials, design, roles, and action.

Beginnings

In the quotation that follows, Michael recalls how playing cops and robbers first began (the game they call casino was developed later). On weekends, the boys' mother works outside the home and their father, as superintendent of the building, is out of the apartment. It's a time, Michael says, "when we are all happy because we're alone, and we could do whatever we want: we could yell, play, and bounce the ball." But even happy times can be boring, and this being the case, Michael sets himself the task of coming up with something for them to do:

> There was two real, real boring Saturdays and Sundays. So me and my brother said: "What we gonna do-oo?" So hot and boring; can't go outside 'cause my mother was working [and] we wake up early.
> So then my brother says, "What can we do?" And I say, "Shut up, let me think." (*I laugh*.) Now like—making/thinking. Then I say, "Hey let's build something with the pillows and blanket!" And he like/oh, I remember/and then we started building like this [the bakery].

Getting the Pillows to Stay in Place

As Michael describes it here, the building process seems simple, even easy: "We just gather some pillows, put them on the floor. Then we take a blanket and put them there on top of the pillows." However, getting soft, pliable material to stay in place is "hard," according to Michael. The very first time they tried, it worked; but when they tried again, the pillows fell and the bakery toppled. In our second conversation, I ask Michael to use what's on hand in the classroom to show me how he goes about building the bakery. So, using three large science textbooks and a trash bag, he demonstrates building design and technique. Similar to the real thing made of pillows and a blanket, the books repeatedly fall. Not until he braces one book against the wall does the structure stand.

When Michael told me that his hands shake as he places the pillows, I was surprised, but kept silent. Putting one pillow next to another did not seem like such a major undertaking to me. Having seen the textbooks fall, however, I am less surprised. Furthermore, I interpret his remark to signify the seriousness with which he takes his efforts to put the stage in place so that the action can begin.

MICHAEL: But sometimes even you do it, it is hard. Like the first time I did it: you know, I tried to build this.
SALLY: Mm hmm.
MICHAEL: Pretty ea-sy. Then it gets hard. I don't know why. Funny, it's supposed to be hard at the beginning then—
SALLY: You mean, the first time you did it, it worked?
MICHAEL: Yeah, it's pretty easy. It didn't take that many tries 'cause it hold/it hold. But then like I keep trying. I don't know, 'cause

sometimes I get nervous when I/I get nervous when I put some stuff down—my hands shake. It is hard to get the pillows down.

Building

Michael took two photographs of the bakery. Photograph 7.1 shows it completed, the money ready to be stolen (in the other bakery photograph not shown here, he captures on film the robber stealing the money).

Michael took eight photographs showing the casino. With the exception that the casino is in a different location in the boys' bedroom, it appears very much like the bakery. Photograph 7.2 shows the early stages of casino building—three pillows are in place; a fourth pillow and the bedcover are yet to be added.

To better understand the similarities of and differences between the two structures Michael builds, I created schematic models using the drawing function of my computer software program. Figure 7.2 shows the bakery viewed from the top and front before the bedcover is added. Figure 7.3 shows the stages of building the casino, with the bedcover added last. Note the differences in number of pillows used: three to make the bakery,

Photo 7.1. The Bakery

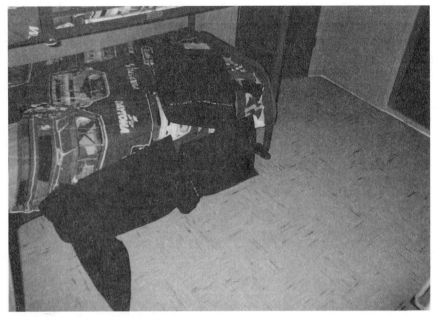

Photo 7.2. Foundation for the Casino

four to make the casino. The bakery is a simpler design, and it appeared first. Additionally, in contrast to the casino, where two gamblers play, the set for cops and robbers need hold only one person—the robber (the store-keeper need not be present), the accused (the judge is, for their purposes, simply an offstage voice), and the jailed robber, in that order.

Referring to the four pillows he uses to make the casino, Michael declares: "That's as wide as we could make it 'cause we don't got no other pillows." The extra pillow used to make the casino goes across the back. The result is a slightly larger interior space than the bakery, which has one pillow across the back. Michael explains in this next quotation how they position themselves inside the casino. It is clear that even with the fourth pillow, it's a very tight fit: "I have to like sit/go like this: you know, my

Figure 7.2. Views of the Bakery

     top view   front view

Figure 7.3. Stages in Building the Casino

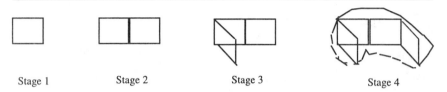

Stage 1   Stage 2   Stage 3   Stage 4

feet [tucked] in. Because if I stretch my feet out, I'll kick my brother's face. And my brother crunch up in here, and I crunch up in here."

When I talked with Michael after his summer vacation, he told me that during this period his father had purchased a "casino set" that came with book, poker chips, dice, and four packs of cards. "He really wanted the book to learn how to play the games," explained Michael, and so he and his brother add the poker chips to their game. With this addition, they decide they need more space: "More space so we could play cards and poker now with the chips." Their solution: with four pillows available, they stay with the original design but separate the two pillows in the back: "I left a big space open." Figure 7.4 shows the new arrangement as viewed from the top and the front.

The boys' bedroom is not air-conditioned. Sometimes, Michael told me, it gets very hot inside the casino. Accordingly, he's made a design adjustment—small openings between blanket and pillow that he dubs "air holes." Even with this improvement, however, he is forced sometimes to poke his head out to take a breath. (As he explains this maneuver, he raises his head, takes a deep breath, and sighs, "Ah-hhh.") Also in the quotation that follows, Michael brings up his recurring problem with the structures he builds; namely, they collapse. He then reports a possible solution.

> I just sometimes I like to stay outside because it gets hot inside [the casino]. And sometimes/like what I said/remember? The blanket sometimes, falls over.
>
> This way, we make up these little things and we put like air holes; and we put like corner here. We twist the pillow a little like

Figure 7.4. Views of the Expanded Casino

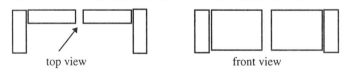

top view   front view

that so some air could come in. 'Cause we get hot. And sometimes we put the fan on the floor . . . We tried that once and it was okay. I was nervous that the fan might blow the pillows in.

THE ACTION

In this section I describe what takes place—the action—when the boys play casino and cops and robbers. Beginning with casino, I describe its origins and follow with how the boys create identities and roles for themselves, direct a crowd scene, effectively modify the set to give it the feel of authenticity, and, working together, develop an entertaining plot. Next, I compare the two games and then turn to cops and robbers to describe its variations.

Origins of Casino

Casino, as the boys refer to it, is a game Michael devised after becoming bored with playing cops and robbers. He explains below how, by combining a fourth pillow and an idea (his), he invented a new game.

> One time, we played the cops and robber game (*he whistles*) lot/a lot of times and I was getting a tiny bit tired. The only thing that I think different is he hides in different spot. So like: "Let's do something else." Then I just did this [pillows and blanket]. And he was like, "It's the same thing, you just put up the thing." And I'm like, "Aw, we have do something different" (*Michael tilts his head upward as if he is thinking*).
> I was thinking of gambling, like, gambling, gambling. "I don't know what to do." Then I was thinking about casino 'cause that's where they mostly gamble. "A gambling casino!" And my brother said: "No-oo, all casinos gamble, real-ly?" So then, but like, like: "What we going to play?" We only could play one 'cause my room is small. We could make it bigger; we could use all the little pillows . . . four.

Casino Play

Under the blanket, "crunched" among the pillows, the boys gamble with dice from their Monopoly game. "Monopoly helps," says Michael. In addition, they use the Monopoly board as a backdrop to throw the dice against instead of the pillows. Even with this precaution, however, there is the danger of the pillows falling over, the casino collapsing, and play stopping.

But when the structure holds, play continues with Michael's brother throwing the dice and asking:

"Mike, how much money do I get?"

"You got a three like that and you got a six. You get three dollars"—something like that. Then he [Allen] just takes the money he gets, puts it down.

The Gamblers

Michael and his brother are, of course, the only two gamblers at their casino. However, as part of the play, they act out an intricate process for gaining entrance to the casino that includes themselves and a line of "imaginary people" (Michael's words). These would-be gamblers, Allen included, must present identification cards at the casino's "door" (see Figure 7.5).

We cut out a piece of paper. . . . We took like the credit card thing. You know, the credit card has those numbers at the bottom. So we took that . . . and we put our address—I don't know why—and our age. 'Cause if guy is 16, he can't go in—you have to be over 21. That's how we do it.

Allen has, I think, about six. I don't know how many he has because he makes different persons. . . . Then one he makes [for] himself: Allen Castro, his real name.

Michael stands by the casino and checks each ID. His brother's ID is the last to be checked:

MICHAEL: Allen goes like down to the kitchen. And it's a long, long line [of people]. Like "You can come in; you can come in; you can't; you can come in; you could go in." Like: "How old are you, kid?"

"I'm 12."

"You're not old enough."

SALLY: What do you mean he goes down to the kitchen? Your kitchen?

MICHAEL: He goes like to the front door [of their apartment]. Then he like, you know, walks. I say, "Take six steps." Just like six people just passed.

Figure 7.5. Allen's Identification Card. The card retains Allen's original drawing, spacing, and age; but the text is typed and the name, address, and phone number have been changed.

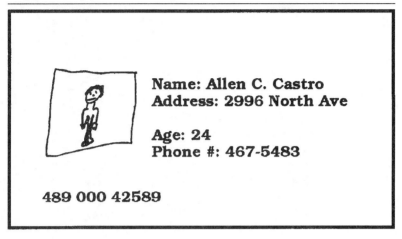

Name: **Allen C. Castro**
Address: **2996 North Ave**

Age: **24**
Phone #: **467-5483**

489 000 42589

And what does Allen do when he's reached the casino door? Michael reports:

> Yeah, he holds his ID—he has it in his back pocket. Then when I say, "ID?" he just flips it out. I think "24" the card says. And I give him back the ID and he comes in. And since I know he's the last person, I go in, too.

The crowd has made their way inside; the gambling can now begin.

COMPARING THE TWO GAMES

Table 7.1 displays five aspects of casino and cops and robbers. Shown are location of their play, the structural materials and designs, the props used, the roles the boys assume, and the action. By comparing and contrasting the two games, we not only see more clearly the similarities of and differences between the two but also uncover more of the inventive qualities of the boys' play—despite the scarity of players, props, and severe limitations of space.

Table 7.1 Comparing Casino with Cops and Robbers

	Casino	*Cops & Robbers*
Location	Structure built on floor next to boys' bunk beds; the gamblers line up in the hallway; play is in bedroom	Built in front of bureau in the boys' bedroom Location of play varies: (1) boys' bedroom (2) all rooms except parents' bedroom (3) all rooms
Materials, design	(1) 4 pillows: 2 across back, 1 on either side; a blanket covers them (2) space between 2 pillows in back	1 pillow across back, 1 on either side; blanket over
Props	- Monopoly $ - game board - dice - IDs	- Monopoly $ - 5 transformers
Roles	- Line of gamblers with IDs - bouncer - gambler - house gambler	- (Victim) - cop - robber - (judge)
Action	Gamblers roll dice and win money	Money is stolen Robber hides Cop looks Robber is found Judge sentences Robber put in jail

The first row in Table 7.1 displays both where the structures are built and where the games are played. We see that although the structures for both games are built in the boys' bedroom, they are located in different parts of that space (refer to Photograph 7.1 and Photograph 7.2). For example, the bakery is built on the floor against a bureau; the casino is also built on the bedroom floor, but it rests against the frame of the lower bunk bed. Casino is played only in the boys' bedroom. In contrast, when conditions are right, cops and robbers extends to other rooms in the apartment—even, on some occasions, to the parents' bedroom. The second row summarizes two interrelated points: the materials used to build the two basic structures and their design. Props, roles, and action—the information given in the remaining three rows—were discussed previously for the game casino. In the section that follows, I describe these aspects for cops and robbers as well as four ways in which the boys vary their play.

COPS AND ROBBERS

The structure built for cops and robbers remains unchanged and in the same place during the course of the game, even though the action changes location. What changes about the structure is what it represents to the boys. Michael sums up: "We got to change the house all the different times. It's got to be the bakery; it's got to be the police station; it has to be the jail cell. It has to be EVERYthing."

Michael took two photographs that pertain to cops and robbers. In the quotation that follows, he reports how he went about it—first he sets up the bakery, adjusts the lights, and locks the door. The latter action is to keep his brother out. He explains: "It was a pain. I had to lock everybody out 'cause my brother wanted to come in. 'Allen, you might get in the way of the picture.'"

Referring me to Photograph 7.1 as we talk, Michael continues along the same lines—namely, the efforts he took to document his play in an accurate manner:

Here is the bakery with the money there. [We] use the Monopoly money . . . [I] have to fold it back so you can see the money. I had to lock the door and turn off the lights so it could look like we playing in the dark . . .

Wishing to photograph a robbery as it is taking place, Michael summons his brother; he recalls:

I said, "Allen, I need you."
  "Why?"
  "I need you as a model. Act like you stealing the money."
  He said, "All right." He act like he took the money.

The photograph Michael takes shows a close-up of Allen playing the part of the robber. The shot taken, Michael remembers saying to Allen: "And I said: 'Now get out of here.'"

The Actors

As the title cops and robbers suggests, there are basically two characters in the game: the cop and the robber. The boys are not much interested in the speaking parts—they want the parts that are fun for them:

SALLY: So who's the cop, the robber, the bakery owner?
MICHAEL: Well, I like to be the robber because it's fun to be sneaky. But I'm mostly the cop. And there really is no bakery owner, we just like imaginary friend.

The action goes like this: The robber sneaks up on the bakery and takes the Monopoly money. The voice of the bakery owner calls out: "Police, police, police." As this next quotation shows, Michael is first the voice of the bakery owner and then the policeman who hears the call:

> Then I make the cop again. And then the cop has to come . . . Then I stop him [the robber]. . . . Then, he don't listen 'cause I don't have a gun. 'Cause my mother doesn't like me playing with guns/toy guns because bad influence. So (*he clears throat*) I just use my finger and I like [say], "Put the money."

With the robber caught, the set—once the bakery—becomes the court-house where the robber is sentenced:

> We make that the courthouse. We make him just stand there. And the judge is right there. And it is like we tell him [the judge] what he did. And he [the judge] just goes like, "Seven years." And he goes "Ding!" (*Michael slams his hand down as if he is holding a gavel*).

The courthouse then becomes the jail:

> Then I just/then I just make this the jail cell and put him in/lock him up . . . I just like throw him in the jail cell. I did that once and the whole jail cell broke down. (*We both laugh*). I had to build it and I put him in GENTly.

(Once again, the problem of the collapsing pillows.) Michael shows me how his brother grips the imaginary bars of his jail cell and calls out plain-tively: "I was framed."

Interested in how they keep cops and robbers going when the only robber is now in jail, I ask:

> SALLY: Does the game start again, or do you stop and start something else?
> MICHAEL: We can't wait to TEN years so we like [say] "Ten years." And then he gets out. And he robs again and again.

To see who will play the robber, the boys toss a coin. And as I will note later, for Michael to enjoy some success as the robber, he insists on changes in timing and lights.

Variations

The boys work to vary the game, but how to do so? Michael describes several solutions: changing the place that is robbed from a small bakery to a large department store, finding more places to hide, using the cover of darkness, and being careful to give the robber time to hide.

The Department Store Robbery. At times when the family's entire apartment is at their creative disposal, the boys make the living room into a large department store, but not without some careful thought. Michael explains:

> I was thinking, then my mind stopped on, "Ah the department store. That's it, the department store!" We could use the house. We make believe the closet/the closet has our clothes. So make believe he be taking the clothes.
>
> We put the money on this like ledge . . . It's like a little ledge sticking out—so we put the money there like that's the cash register or, I mean, the cashier, whatever, but there's nobody there. So we just put/leave the money there, make believe he take the clothes.
>
> And the more fun is, we get to hide wherever we want. 'Cause my father doesn't know. He doesn't let us hide in his room. If he catches us, we're dead meat; we're in trouble; we're going to be punished.

Question: How will the cop know a crime has been committed so that the chase can begin? The boys' solution: The department store comes with its own alarm system.

> MICHAEL: You know those things like under the table and they push
>   it? Looks like a real button. It's like silent. They use it in the banks.
> SALLY: Like an alarm? I'm not sure who hears it.
> MICHAEL: Yeah, I think it goes for the cops. We just make it like that.

(Now I get it! The robbery takes place in the living room and, meanwhile, the cop is eating a doughnut in the bedroom.) A sound alerts the cop to spring into action:

> SALLY: So you're sitting there eating your doughnut, but you hear
>   it?
> MICHAEL: I'm like "Uh oh!" Just drop my doughnut and get in my
>   car, and I start going.

More Places to Hide. Michael says about having more places for the robber to hide, "It's more, I don't know, it feels like it's more exciting." He recalls the time when it seemed as if his brother had simply disappeared. He looked for his brother in the usual places, then went back to the police station in their bedroom:

> So then I look for him. . . . So I'm going looking under the b-ed (he draws the sound out), and the clo-set, behind the curtains and everything. And I was like, "Where could he be?"
>
> Then I hear something like some noise. 'Cause he like, I think he coughed—I don't know (*he pauses*). But then I still ain't know where he was. So I went back to my room. It was like "Probably was a false call."

When he hears another sound, Michael leaves the bedroom. He glimpses his brother this time and stops the game by calling "time out." When Michael asks for the hiding place, his brother offers a cliché; when pressed, he gives another answer that seems just as implausible.

> I see my little brother running into the kitchen. I'm like, "Where could he be?" I'm like, "Allen, Allen, time out, time out" (*he laughs*). "Where were you?" Like [I think] "It's a secret passage." I'm like, "[But] there's like NO secret passages in the wall!" "Where were you?"
>
> "I was in the hamper."
>
> "You are a LIar!"

To see for himself, Michael follows his brother into the bathroom. But before his brother will get into the hamper, he makes Michael "swear to God" that he won't shut him inside. Michael explains what happens next: "And then he went all the way in . . . And I tried to do that myself but my butt wouldn't fit."

Under the Cover of Darkness. Another variation in their play when they are home alone is to turn off the lights. This is most effective at night:

> And when we play at night, we play like the department store is closed. So it's harder. So he goes, he breaks in there; he just takes all the money. There's no lady there [for him] to say [to], "Put the money in the bag." He just grabs it and puts it in his pocket.
>
> When we turn off the lights, it's really really really REALLY dark. And that's when it gets more harder. It takes me like maybe 10, 15 minutes to find him.

From Michael's point of view, playing in the dark means that he has more chances to hide successfully even though he is much taller than his brother: "In the dark . . . can't see nobody, no matter how big they are—10 feet tall." When they don't play in the dark, Michael, playing the part of the robber, negotiates for extra time to hide. But as he sees it, playing in the dark puts his brother and himself on more equal terms.

> He goes inside [police station], acts like he's eating his doughnut, and I run and hide. He gives me a little extra time 'cause I'm more bigger and have to find a good hiding spot. He find me easy. But in the DARK, we never find each other, we mostly have to give up.

Time to Hide. The issue of how much time the policeman gives the robber to hide before the search begins is a critical one. Michael says: "We have to give it a little extra time . . . It wouldn't be right if I just go, 'Okay, ready or not, here I come.'" Interestingly, by giving the same structure multiple functions, they change the timing of their play and make it not only more fair for the robber but more exciting for all. Michael explains:

> The first time we ever made the game up, I had to be in the bed so that could be the bakery. But we ain't think about making that the courthouse or the jail cell. So as soon as he ran away from the bakery, I say, "Calling all cars," and I would just run.

Without sufficient wait time, the robber cannot hide and is soon caught. Once again, as the next quotation shows, Michael comes to the rescue with an idea:

> "That's not fair 'cause you could just chase me." And I'm like: "All right, I got it, this could be/now, as soon as you leave, this could be the police station.
>   "Okay. I'll be eating my doughnut. Then I'll just wait for like/I'll give you 25 seconds." (*He puts hand to mouth as if eating, each chewing action counting as a second.*) After 25 seconds, "Calling all cars."

Clues

When Michael and I talk after summer vacation, he tells me that over the summer they changed cops and robbers by making the policeman search the house for "clues" before he can search for the robber. "I made it/I made it up," he says, giving himself full credit. As a result, there are more things to look for and "this way," appraises Michael, "we make it a lot more challenging."

Michael tells me that this extension was stimulated by his repeating to himself: "I have to get the five clues before I find Allen." He clarifies: "Like if I'm the cop—my brother hides the objects. I have to find them." The objects are five small toys (called "transformers"). The robber hides them in different places: "I hide the toys where I want. Like I hide them behind the canister in the freezer," Michael explains. But to make sure I understand what's been added or changed to the older version, I ask: "But what's the sequence?"

Michael patiently continues: "Okay, I'm sitting down eating my doughnut. Allen robs the place. I find out. He runs. I give him time to hide the objects and hide. Hides objects, goes hide where he wants to. I walk. Find one."

Michael names four of the five clues, as follows: a murder weapon,[1] the glove and mask the robber wore, and the robber's fingerprints. Without them all, the cop cannot identify the robber. Hence, they may actually pass each other "in the street":

> If I see 'im, I can't do nothing. So he like/we could walk right by each other and I can't do nothing . . . because I don't have the evidence . . . It could be/we act like there's people walking by. He could be like an innocent person, but he's really the bad person.

As Michael explains next, he's fooled his brother by pretending that he did not have the necessary five clues in his possession before making the arrest. By keeping one clue hidden, Michael pretends to make a mistake. As it turns out, however, it's the robber who's badly mistaken.

> I put one in my pocket sometimes and I have four [visible]. I'm walking and Allen sees me. "I got you!" [I say to him.] "Ah, but you only have four of them," [Allen replies.] I take out the other one (*Michael moves his hand as if he's taking something out of his pocket*).
> "Oh, you cheated, you cheated!" [says Allen, the robber, accusingly].
> "No [replies Michael the cop], I can't hold them all."

I'm still not convinced how the cop knows who to arrest, so I ask: "But how would you know Allen is the robber?" I'm told that the evidence is so strong that often the robber confesses. Michael explains:

---

1. This is the first I'd heard of a murder. At the time I didn't ask any follow-up questions. I interpret the "murder weapon" as going with the "scene of the crime" leitmotif rather than what happens in his version.

Well, I act like I put all the evidence: "Glove (*his voice changes*); fingerprints. I know this guy, I arrested him last year. There he goes." Run, look. "Gotcha." I have to show him the five evidence 'cause I could just be like, "I found the five evidence or five things." "Man" [the thwarted robber's reply].

In the quotation that follows, Michael provides a summary and deals with the reality of having only one suspect:

MICHAEL: And when we find 'em [the clues], I know exactly who the person is . . . Well, I really know who it is because there's only person who is playing with me. (*I laugh.*) But if he walks by me as the cop, I don't know it.

SALLY: Hmm. Seems much more true to life.

MICHAEL: It is. As I've gotten older, I've got better games.

CONCLUSION

The most important factor determining what the boys play and where is not the small space or the lack of props, but their parents. According to the boys, more vigorous, expansive, and, consequently, exciting play is only possible when their parents are away, as Michael reiterates:

We use the whole house, not just my room. 'Cause my room, well, it's big, but I'm saying, it's a little small 'cause it don't have that many hiding spots. And if I go to hide, I have to leave the room. [And if] Allen's like in the closet, I just open the door—and there he is. So we just use like the whole house.

Hence, the Sunday matinees that Michael directs and stars in are best played to an empty house. His is a low-budget thriller that works best when the lights are out. In Michael's plays, actors follow basic scripts, but he rewrites them. Challenged by boredom and routine, he comes up with a new game or a variation on an old one; suffocating, he invents air holes; crunched, he designs a larger setting; having but one location for all the action, he simply names it something else and yells, "ACTION!"; and with a cast of only two actors, the boys play multiple roles.

To know what is *supposed* to happen, Michael relies partly on what he's seen in movies and on television and imitates that. These sources provide him not only with the "usual" characters, dialogue, and plot but with images and sounds—the setting. He also relies on direct and indirect ex-

periences with bakeries, departments stores, casinos, the police, and rob-
beries. For example, since he was not yet 21, Michael reminded me that
he had never been to a casino himself but had seen what it looks like on
the television sitcom "Roseanne."

Michael is imitating and pretending, but what he does and how he does
it are a consequence of his power to think, create, and solve problems.
When he talks about what they do when they play, he says: "We thought,"
"I . . . invent," "I'm very intelligent," "We were thinking," "My mind
stopped [on an idea]," "I just made them up," "I made it/I made it up,"
"We just made it up," "This could be."

In the give-and-take in Michael's head and the exchange between the
brothers, stories, sets, and action are created and evolve:

> Allen invented the cops and robber game like that. I invented the
> one about the/I invented the bakery . . . He said, "Why don't we
> play cops and robbers?" and I said, "How we going to do that?" Then
> he just told me how we were going to do it. Then I just said, "This
> could be like the bakery sometime. This could be—or stuff like that."

Hence, when Michael says "As I've gotten older, I've got better games,"
he acknowledges his ability to have ideas and to improve them, to build
upon and out of multiple experiences, to experiment and make changes,
to expand or retract depending on local factors, conditions, and resources.
In the matter of play and games, he gives himself credit as someone who
makes things up, makes things happen.

8 REX: A Temporary Retreat

Well, sometimes in the winter—this started when I was about 8 years old. Once I was really cold. And I just/I just thought of something. I just got a sheet (*he pauses*) to try to keep warm. And I put it just like the way it is in the picture that I just told you about—like right here. And I put the sheet right there and the other chair, the rocking chair, right there . . . And I turn on the heater and act like it's Eskimo.

Rex explains in the above quotation how, one winter when he was feeling "really cold," he thought of draping a sheet between two chairs placed near each other in the family's living room, as shown in his drawing (see Figure 8.1). Getting underneath and staying "real close" to a heater, he kept himself warm.

Rex's drawing is reduced to fit the page of this book, but his attention to detail and his naming things aid explanation. For example, the line drawn on the right side denotes a living room wall. Shown against this wall—as he has labeled them—are rocking chair, heater, chair, and plants. Covering the heater and chair is a sheet, and next to this enclosure is the family cat, whose name is given in parenthesis (Evan). Shown against the wall at the bottom of the drawing, unlabeled, is a sofa. Rex draws two large cabinets against the upper wall—one with open shelves and the other with doors. He labels the former a "wall unit" and has drawn a "super Nintendo," a TV, and a computer on its shelves. On top of the second cabinet are trophies. Rex draws these cabinets, the furniture on the right, and the cat as if we were facing them. In contrast, the chairs, sheet, and heater appear to be drawn as if we are looking down at them (similarly, an aerial perspective appears in the photographs he takes—what he will call a "blimp mode").

Figure 8.1. Rex's Drawing

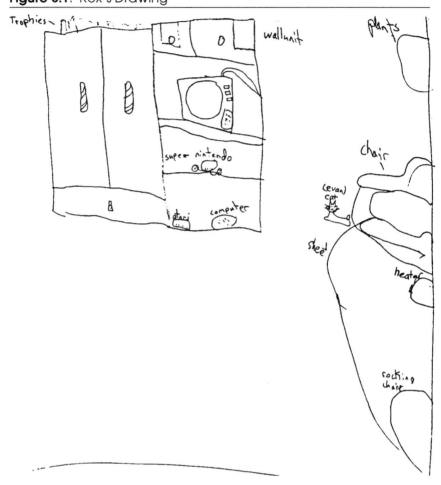

Now 10 years old and a fifth grader, Rex reports that he continues to "act like a kind of Eskimo," as he puts it, when he is cold, bored, or both. He shares an apartment with his mother and an older brother; both work. The apartment is on the fifth floor of a building recently renovated by a local church group. Rex sits under a sheet in the family's living room when he is alone; it is his secret:

SALLY: So I guess your mom knows about what you build, right?
REX: No, she don't know about it.

SALLY: So you do it when she's not around?
REX: She usually at work.
SALLY: I see. So this is really a secret?
REX: (*His shoulders go up.*) Yeah, I guess.

I will return to Rex indoors, but first I will move briskly through his outdoor play to describe how he and his friends attempted the previous winter to build a "little dome . . . kind of like an Eskimo thing" with snow. By considering what Rex does and plays *outdoors*, we will see what most people see: the fast-paced, competitive, often warlike play among boys of mixed ages. In contrast, when we return to Rex's descriptions of what he does and plays alone *indoors*, we are permitted to glimpse the private, sheltered world he builds for himself. Outdoors and indoors, he may build "like an Eskimo thing," but they are worlds apart.

REX OUTDOORS

Because Rex is taller than most other boys his age, he looks older than he is, and that, he says, puts him at a disadvantage:

REX: I'm 10 years old. People think I'm really like 13 years old—but I'm only 10. So that's kind of a setback.
SALLY: Why is that a "setback"?
REX: 'Cause when I play basketball, people always think I'm older. So they gonna try to play hard and all of that, you know.

Aiming, throwing, running, jumping, and "playing hard" are prominent features in the sports and games Rex plays outdoors with other boys—some older, some younger—who live on his block. When repeated snowfalls the previous winter covered streets, sidewalks, and cars, Rex and his small group of friends took advantage of the stockpile for their play. First to be described is a "fort" the boys built during an extended snowball fight. Technically more like a rampart, the mound of snow offers protection yet allows the boys to freely throw their missiles from one side of the street to the other. At another time, when not at war, the same boys will try to build a more igloo-like structure—one with a top.

The "Real Big" Snowball Fight

In the long quotation that follows, Rex reports skirmishes and battles and the building of a snow fort during the previous winter. By choosing words that convey movement and action, he is both sportscaster and war correspondent, providing commentary on who, what, when, and where:

> In winter there was/we had like this snowball fight—it was real big.
> It went on from something like 12 o'clock in the morning—I mean
> at noon until about 10:30 at night. We were just going crazy.
>
> There was like this little brick wall. And me, my friend Jason,
> José and Samuel, my friend José and Samuel, we/we was behind it.
> And we was throwing stuff. Then Mark, he was on the other side—
> he was like 16 years old. He just came and hit me in the back of the
> head—out of nowhere.
>
> Then I got up, and I started running after him. Then Randy, who
> was on the other side, he threw another snowball at me. Then I had
> to run all the way to my building. I came back out—about 2 minutes
> later. I ran behind this car. That's when I built that little fort. It was
> about to here (*he measures about 4 feet with his hands*).

In the next section, I describe the efforts of Rex and his friends to build another snow structure—one with a top. Although building material (snow) is plentiful, problems in location and design must be solved.

"Kind of Like an Eskimo Thing"

According to Rex, they start building between parked cars. They are forced to move their base of operations when car owners start moving their cars:

> We started from the bumper—the back bumper of the car. And
> started piling a lot. Eventually the cars kept moving out . . . The/the
> guy was/he was all complaining to us. Said I have to move it. And
> we went to this other one. It's next to this church on our block.

The place they choose for their second attempt offers protection from the wind, as Rex explains: "'Cause it was like SOLid right here. So only this wind . . . it just coming in like from one little side."

Building with Snow. I ask Rex to clarify what he means by "kind of like an Eskimo thing" when describing the structure they build. "Like an igloo?" I ask. But his response—"Yeah, a little hole under it"—leaves me baffled. I am still unsure if a hole was carved out of piled-up snow or if snow was piled around an open space.

> REX: We just piled it around it. Once we made like this, we tried to
> clamp snow on top of each other.

SALLY: Like you're making a huge snowball?

REX: Yeah, but without the center.

SALLY: Without the center. Eventually without the center. You started with a huge snowball and then dug out the center?

REX: No. We built it from the sides and went up to about here; then we took the snow all around it (*he shows how he formed the snow with his hands*) 'til/until finally we got around.

At my urging, he patiently tries again and I understand:

We just took a whole bunch of snow. We piled it up kinda like a snowball—a big snowball. Then we kinda like/tried to put a hole in it. But as we put a hole in it, snow was kind of like falling down from the top when we got inside . . . When we went in, it just fell on us.

The location of the hole puzzles me next. The "little hole" Rex talks about may refer to a hole they make at the top, as is typically shown in pictures of igloos, or to a hole in the side, near the base, to allow someone to enter. I assume the latter because I'm told that the boys crawl inside— but only "for about 10 seconds" because the "little dome" collapses around them.

My trying to make sense of how they built the "little dome" and what it looked like continued into our fourth conversation. Again responding to my request, while at the same time correcting my inaccuracies, Rex describes how two low brick walls at the site are integral to the construction process. In the explanation that follows, we also glimpse how Rex thinks in terms of mathematical concepts and uses them to help solve problems of design and technology.

REX: It was like, there was this brick wall—it was about this tall (*he raises his hand about 3 feet from the floor*). And we just had it/it [the snow piles] go kinda higher. Be like kind of a igloo.

SALLY: Oh, so you had two walls maybe?

REX: Yeah.

SALLY: At right angles?

REX: Just one right angle.

They pile and pack snow higher and higher, paying close attention to "building it around." By making the walls rounded and building up and up until the sides meet, they try to avoid both the difficulties of making "little angles" and of making a roof that is flat. Rex explains the process and his reasoning:

REX: If it were like square, it would be hard to make—like all these
little angles and everything. And if you try to make it square, it
easily fall in on us—'cause like flat (*he turns his hand face down and
a couple of inches off the table*).
SALLY: Oh, you didn't want a flat roof?
REX: Like snow would hit it (*he takes his other hand and hits the one
representing the roof, pushing that hand down*).
SALLY: Right.
REX: So if we made it like a dome, it would like tip it to the side a
little bit, you know.

If the "Little Dome" Had Stood. When I ask Rex about what they expected to do once inside, he answers:

REX: We was just going to go in there (*he pauses*). It wasn't that big
though.
SALLY: Could everybody have fit?
REX: I guess so. Be squished though. We were going to like hang in
there just like/I don't know—just do stuff in there.

Because the boys' stay inside the little dome is brief, we do not have a
very good idea of what "like hang in there" looks like. We can assume that
because this is no huge "superdome," their usual sports activities are an
impossibility; hence, new play and games would have to be invented or
old ones adapted. There are, however, some clues regarding what "stuff"
might have happened inside the little dome in what Rex remembers about
a book his teacher shared with his class. In the quotation that follows, his
emphasis is on warmth and safety:

She brought this book about this Eskimo—this little Eskimo girl.
And they had like a little top open. So they would have a fire and
everything—with a bear rug. So it'll be heat—but won't be all
smoke; won't kill 'em.

REX INDOORS

The photographs Rex took show a living room very much like the one he
drew for me at our first meeting; it is furnished with matching chairs (they
look large and sturdy), a cabinet, and a wall unit on the shelves of which
are a TV and equipment for playing Nintendo. The photographs also show

that at least two shelves in the wall unit are devoted to children—their awards and prized things they have made. For example, next to a certificate for "Achievement in Science" is one saying "Honor Roll." Also on these shelves are a child's drawing and a woman's name spelled out in wooden letters (a child's project made in school or summer camp?). To the left of the wall unit is another cabinet; on top of it—again, as in Rex's drawing—are trophies (but I am unsure which of these and the other personal items belong to Rex, to his older brother, or to both boys).

My focus in this section is on what Rex builds indoors. My impression is that Rex sees his friends more frequently outside than inside, either at his apartment or at theirs. He does mention, however, playing hide-and-seek indoors with two friends. By comparison, he recalls play when he was younger as more frequent and more imaginative:

> I used to/I used to have an imagination—but it's not that cra-zy. I used to imagine that I was like a Ninja and stuff. And I also go under the bed and stuff and pretend it was a kind of fort. That was way back when I was about 6 though.

To the extent that the indoor games Rex lists are active, physical, and competitive, they are similar to the sports and games he plays outside. I turn now to the seemingly quieter, more passive activities he does when alone indoors. The focus is on the structure he makes in his living room. Instead of snow and ice, he uses a sheet or a blanket and two chairs. Instead of a bear rug and a fire, he stays close to a heater. Instead of being with friends, he is alone except for his cat.

Acting "Like a Kind of Eskimo"

Rex does not name what he builds indoors. Instead, he names himself when inside—he is "a kind of Eskimo":

> Sometimes when I'm in my house—and I'm bored or something—I have like/take a sheet or something and I turn on my heater. When I'm cold. Then I put that like around my heater. Then I act like a kind of Eskimo or something.

Rex does, however, distinguish between what he builds when he acts "kind of like an Eskimo" and when he builds a "tent." He sees the similarity but clearly makes a distinction. As he explains:

> REX: And sometimes like I'll put like/try to hold it up—so it could be like a tent—a little bit. I only do that a little bit of times though.

SALLY: Hmm?
REX: I only do that like (*he pauses*) once in a blue moon.

I press him to name what he builds. If it is like a tent, but not a tent, then what is it? I press on:

SALLY: What do you call this when you build it? What do you think
     to yourself?
REX: It doesn't really like have a name (*he puts his shoulders up as if to
     say, "I don't know"*).
SALLY: Doesn't have a name.
REX: I just build it.

Sitting Under the Sheet

Like his drawing (refer to Figure 8.1), Rex's photographs show his attentiveness to where things are located in his living room and in what relation to each other. Photographs he took show, for instance, how he stretches a sheet between the arms of two chairs and tucks one edge of it under the double doors of the china cabinet to hold it in place (see Photo 8.1). Missing from an otherwise thorough picture of the set-up is Rex. Because he took all the photos, we don't get to see him either making the structure or inside it.

Unlike Brenda, Rex does not eat inside the structure he makes. Also unlike Brenda, who very much wants a pet dog, Rex has a cat named Evan that he sometimes brings inside with him. Rex did not take a photograph of his cat; but she does appear in his drawing, and his detailed description of what she looks like seems to show not only his attention to her appearance but also her importance to him.

She looks um/it's black fur, black stripes and gray stripes mixed
together. Like black gray, black gray. And her face is gray and black
also. Her nose is—all cats' nose is pink. She looks like a regular cat
. . . And right here is all white. Some of it is like black right here.

As both the drawing and photographs show, Rex can sit under the sheet and, from this vantage point, see the television set in the wall unit. But to do so, as he tells me, he has to "pick up the blanket a little bit." He speaks of sometimes playing at being a sniper or a Ninja, making watching television a kind of interactive process:

REX: Sometimes I try to ah/act like I'm some kind of sniper or
     something.

Photo 8.1. What Rex Builds

SALLY: Mm hmm.
REX: Trying to watch TV or stuff or Ninja. And I like doing stuff. Kind of act like some kind of war.
SALLY: Mm hmm. So do you bring like a toy gun or something inside?
REX: Yeah, sometimes.

Origins and Originality

I turn now to what Rex says about himself when I ask him about the origins of his indoor building activities. His responses consistently include a story. The first is about how he got the nickname "Rocky"; the second is an explanation of why his mother says he is "smart." In both instances, he tells me not so much about the origins of the structure as about how others see him—a boy on his own, resilient and imaginative.

SALLY: And how in the world did you learn how to do it [build your structure]? I mean, like, where did this idea come from?
REX: I don't know. One day it was just like kinda real cold so I just did it.

This response is weather-related. But as my next question suggests, I am after the person or idea that sparked his work; in so doing, I assume that inspiration can be named, pegged, and comes from without. It's a view, with Rex's assistance, that I modify.

> SALLY: And you've never seen this before? Like your older brother didn't teach you how to do it? (*He shakes head "No."*) So you just kind of made it up?
> REX: Yeah, kind of (*he pauses*). My family calls me "Rocky"— that's my nickname.
> SALLY: Rocky? [I am unsure of the direction the conversation seems to be taking, not the correctness of his nickname.]
> REX: That's my nickname.
> SALLY: And why/how did you get that nickname?
> REX: 'Cause when I was a baby sometimes I used to climb out of my crib; then I fell on my head or something. They'd say my head is hard like a rock. So named me "Rocky."

In the previous quotation and in the one that follows, Rex's initial reply to my question about origins is an "I don't know" expressed in both words and body language. I persist in the first instance and, inadvertently, make a reference to his family. He then responds with how his family views him. In the first example and in the one that follows, it's his head that is the focus of attention—first for its capacity to withstand hard knocks and then for its capacity to have ideas.

> SALLY: So you just kind of made the structure up? (*Rex's shoulders go up as if to say, "I don't know."*) Did somebody else in the family—
> REX: Nope, I just went about it.
> SALLY: But then you had to figure out where to do it, what to use.
> REX: Not really, it just came inside my head.
> SALLY: Okay.
> REX: My mother says that I'm like smart in all of this.

That Rex thinks what he does is unique also comes out when I ask him if he thinks other children build as he does. He speaks to the singularity of his play, as follows:

> REX: To me it's unusual.
> SALLY: Uh huh. How 'bout some of your friends, when they come over, do you ever do this? (*Rex shakes his head to signify "No."*) Hmm. I wonder though if other kids don't do it.
> REX: I don't think other kids will do that.

VIEWPOINTS

Rex is able to think about himself; in other words, to see himself as others see him. His ability to use perspective comes up again when he talks about the photographs he has taken. First, I will share some of his perspective-taking as a photographer. Next, I turn to his imagining past and future selves—another kind of perspective taking.

Angles and Aerial Shots

With the disposable camera I gave him to document what he builds, Rex took a total of eleven pictures of his living room, including five of the structure he builds there (three with a sheet; two with a blanket). Before he took the camera home, we talked about what he might photograph and I recall standing on a chair to demonstrate how he might take some shots. When he talks about his photographs, Rex refers over and over again to *how* he took a picture: specifically, he refers to views and angles, positioning, close-ups, and lighting. For example, in the quotation that follows, Rex quickly describes one photograph, then another. He begins with the "aerial" shot he took of chairs and heater and then reports that he stood behind the couch to get the next shot. He adds that the brightness of the room makes the TV screen difficult to see. "This is from the other arm of the chair. This is another blimp mode, but I'm closer. And this is, I'm behind the couch. And you can see the TV on a little bit 'cause the light is too much."

In summary, Rex is meticulous in photographing the structure he builds in his family's living room. He takes different positions around the room and even stands on the arm of a chair to get the pictures he wants. In addition, he takes pictures of the space between the chairs both with and without the sheet in place.

But with all his attention to detail and perspective, Rex does not take any shots from inside the structure. (In this he is like the other children who took photographs.) I can think of four explanations: He didn't think to do so; he thought to, but for some reason decided against it; he saw his task as documenting what a visitor—me, for instance—would see; or he received no suggestion from me to do so (I thought to ask only Brenda to take pictures from inside the structures she built, looking out).

Disclosures

The focus in this section is on what Rex says he does when under the sheet. The majority of the dialogue that follows comes from our second conversation. This interview turned out to be our longest, seemingly most wide-ranging, possibly most revealing, and certainly most uncomfortable for me. Let me try to explain this feeling of discomfort before returning to the substance of the conversation.

My Discomfort. Of all the children I talked with for this study, it was with Rex that I felt most uncomfortable. Why? I felt pushy. When he responded to my questions by hunkering up his shoulders and saying, "I don't know, I just . . . ," instead of waiting or simply accepting this response, I often persisted. For instance, I asked him to name what he builds and to give labels to his feelings.

Another way of saying I felt uncomfortable is to say that I felt "self-conscious" with Rex. Unlike the other children with whom I talked for this study, with Rex I was aware of having an agenda and aware that the interview process was, even at its best, an artificial means of engaging him in thinking and talking. However, despite what I am calling my pushiness, I think I also came across as someone genuinely interested in him, someone who wanted to know him better. I will return to this point later.

Rex's View of the Future. In an earlier quotation, Rex talks about other people seeing him as older than he really is. When playing basketball, for example, people thinking he is 13 when he is really 10 is a "setback," or disadvantage, for him because "they gonna try to play hard." On and off the basketball court, others think about him and form opinions; it makes things hard for him if what they perceive is not his view.

Our second conversation begins when I ask him what kinds of things he does and thinks about when sitting under the sheet. My question is a general one; Rex answers that he thinks about himself in the future—what he will be when he grows up. I then ask why he does his thinking under the sheet and not in some other place (e.g., on his bed or on the sofa). He responds: "I just want to relax when I'm there. Like I'm isolated from the rest of the world; you know, no distractions and stuff."

My response is to share where I feel away from "distractions and stuff"; namely, my bathtub. As I speak, I feel I may be saying something inappropriate in my attempt to show him that we have something in common, so I quickly ask him what he thinks about when he thinks about the future. In doing this, I am picking up on some earlier comments he made regarding what he will be when he grows up. However, he tells me not about his future self but about who he might have been in the past: "I think about what I used to be or something that I'm probably reincarnated or something . . . Like sometimes I still believe in that lost city of Atlantis. I think I used to be some kind of animal in it."

I listen, respond with "Uh huh," and then continue with my earlier line of questioning related to his thoughts about the future. I ask, "Do you think like a year ahead?" Rex responds by telling me what happened the night before. What he relates is part actual happening and part dream—entering an actual video contest and refusing his mother's advice mixed with a dream set in the future in which he is a video game entrepreneur who invents a monster that kills him.

Rex's Dream. That Rex would tell me about a dream he had surprised me. I have tried to make sense of it in the context of our conversations in general and his worldmaking activity in particular. In our previous conversations, he seemed reticent to talk about himself, answering instead with an "I don't know," a shrug, or both. The dream sequence, moreover, is long and rich in images—far more so than any descriptions of what he does and thinks about when sitting under the sheet. Below is our conversation in full; I follow with my thinking about the possible importance for Rex of my listening to him.

SALLY: Let's see, next year you'll be in the sixth grade. Do you think like a year ahead?

REX: Sometimes I think about that. Last night I had a dream. Last night at about 10 o'clock I signed up for a tournament. And I had a dream that I was the winner and everything. And it was like the year 2010, and I owned this big video game company.

SALLY: Uh huh.

REX: And then all of a sudden then the game came alive and killed me.

SALLY: What?

REX: I made this killer game, and one of the characters from the game came out and killed me.

SALLY: E-E-E-E. You mean you had won the game and then you—

REX: I had made this sequel to it. It was like—I can't remember what it was called 'cause sometimes when I have a/the dream was kind of deep so I can't really remember what.

SALLY: Deep?

REX: So I can't really remember what happened, but it was like this guy, um, you know about that game, Mortal Combat? [a video game]

SALLY: No.

REX: Anyway, it has this guy called Cano and the guy came out with his knife. (*He makes slashing motion.*) Ay—

SALLY: That was in your dream? Did you wake up?

REX: [?] still dreaming.

SALLY: What happened, did you become reincarnated in your dream?

REX: No. Like the cops came. My body just stayed there with the head right next to the body.

SALLY: So you were dreaming about yourself (*I pause*) being dead?

REX: Pretty much. Because I'm not all kind of nervous. 'Cause my mother/she will like: "You're going to win; don't be nervous." Ahhh. But you have to be kind of nervous so it gives you that (*he pauses*) extra edge. So you must practice a little harder.

SALLY: Uh huh. What was your mother urging you to do last night?

REX: She just kept saying, "Always be confident in yourself. Don't be nervous or you do worse." Blah, blah, blah, blah, blah, blah, blah (*he pauses*). I don't like that.

SALLY: Uh huh. Well, Rex, if you're feeling nervous, you're feeling nervous. Right? And you know you're feeling nervous and—

REX: You can't really just stop that; you have to like take yourself step by step with that nervous thing.

SALLY: Did you figure that out yourself that you have to take it "step by step"?

REX: I feel kind of nervous when I think about it a lot. I think about what might happen. I might not make it past the first round or something.

I wonder if I may have misunderstood the importance for Rex of my being an adult who listened to him in a nonjudgmental and nonevaluative way. Moreover, it may be my mistake to see his dream as a revelation more personal and private than his telling me about his outdoor play, his indoor play when younger, or what he daydreams about while sitting under the sheet. I also failed to see his "I don't know" and shrug as honest answers; to realize that rather than being evasive, he had never before been asked to explain himself. Thus, it may be that all along Rex was confiding in me. When I ask why he thinks it important for adults to know about children's play, his response focuses on the need for "better conversations" between parent and child, but I see myself and other adults included here as well:

SALLY: Why should adults know about children's play?

REX: So they could know them better. If they want to have a conversation, they could have a better conversation with their child.

REVELATION VERSUS EXPOSURE

As I said earlier, the above sequence surprised me. I could see how his signing up for a local video game contest might trigger anxiety that would find expression in a dream, but I did not readily connect this dream to my questions concerning what he thinks about when sitting under the sheet in his living room. The connection remains tenuous but here is one possibility: An underlying theme in both is control. Let me explain. Following the previous quotation, I ask six questions related to where this contest is taking place; to my last question, "So you've done these before?" Rex shakes his head says, "I just do this at my house." He then continues: "In the winter—I want to go back to another subject. In winter there was/we had like this snowball fight—it was real big."

With that beginning, he tells me again—as he did in our first conversation—about a snowball fight and building "that little fort." Perhaps the positioning here of "I want to go back to another subject" signifies his desire for some relief. However, much of what I said earlier about the winter story applies here to the dream sequence. Both are action dramas; both are rich in images of war. Rex gives a sense of place in his winter tale, but not in the dream; but in both I feel as if the players and characters are suspended in time—that is, in a world of their own.

In the "real big" snowball fight sequence, Rex reports that he is hit and must seek sanctuary, but he returns—to build a shelter. In contrast, we learn in his dream that even a carefully constructed sequel can turn into a nightmare. In this instance, a character comes out of a video game and slays his creator. By linking dream to video game contest, he comes up with a list of maxims when things are out of control. These maxims are: Do not trust the advice of adults; life is a series of steps; take each step one at a time; nevertheless, some never get past the first round. What seems consistent in both the dream and the winter tale is the theme of being and not being in control of events, being and not being in control of one's world.

Finally, the dream sequence falls in the genre of an action adventure and as such is likely to come across as vivid and lively in the retelling. In comparison, what Rex does when under the sheet comes across as reflective and passive, bordering on no action at all. The action is in the thinking, the imagining of a possible self: "I just think about what I gonna be; what I'm gonna be; what I might be—when I grow up."

When I ask him if he might build a similar structure for himself outdoors, he says quickly:

REX: Kind of embarrassing if you do that in public.
SALLY: Why would it be embarrassing?

REX: Everybody's all staring at you.

SALLY: Uh huh. But they wouldn't see you.

REX: Well, they like be walking by and I come out or something.

Running, throwing snowballs, building a snow fort, and getting inside it with your friends is okay to do. Being seen sitting under a sheet alone is not. You would be stared at, and that's embarrassing. Better now to have two selves: a public, exterior self open to inspection, and a private, interior self closed off and hidden, "isolated from the rest of the world."

Rex has built himself a kind of incubator, where, protected and apart from family and the crowd, he can safely make his plans, control the situation, and dream his future. It is not yet time for him to move from his offstage location and be his full self "in public." As he told me, "you have to like take yourself step by step." I do so want him to "make it past the first round."

CONCLUSION

Lessons for Adults

With this book, I try to begin to bridge critical gaps in the research literature on what children in middle childhood do and play; to do so, I have focused on the three-dimensional structures city kids build and then play inside. In this final chapter, I explain what I have learned from my research and go on to suggest how these findings relate to the everyday work of educators, specifically those who teach in urban schools. I conclude more generally with the need for all adults to engage in improving and building community.

LESSONS I LEARNED

Believing that research methods in themselves can reify stereotypes, I designed multiple data-collection methods that built on children's capacities to describe and give meaning to their experiences. I asked the children to draw, document with photographs, and talk with me about the worlds they create indoors in apartments and hallways and outdoors in the shared spaces of playgrounds, parks, vacant lots, stoops, and sidewalks. By looking at the three-dimensional structures six children built in an urban environment, I entered—to some extent—the worlds city kids build for and by themselves.

Having worked with children for many years in informal educational settings (including after-school programs for youth and a museum visited by school groups and families), I was not surprised that Brenda, Isaac, Michelle, Ayisha, Rex, and Michael were "full of beans." I learned about their skill in transforming environments, using and adapting objects for their own purposes; at their ability and skill to use as source material for their play what they've heard about in school, read in books, and seen in movies and on television. I learned that they take their play seriously, describing activities as intentional and purposeful that others see only as ordinary and simplistic. I learned about the significance they give to friendship and having a best friend. Finally, I learned about their ability—despite constraints and limitations—to imagine and then construct complex worlds in which they author the scripts, build and manage the sets, and are the stars. Below, I describe in more detail six aspects of the children's worldmaking.

"We Put Our Minds to It." When the children talk about the three-dimensional structures they build, they portray themselves as builders and thinkers. Their ability to re-create the world is shown in their making a place for themselves where there was no place for them. The children take their efforts as worldmakers seriously and see the work as an ongoing process. As Brenda explains: "I have like a book with me and a pencil, and I'm thinking about another way I could do a teepee." Ayisha sums up their achievements: "This shows you what we was imagining . . . and would look like if we put our minds to it." Brenda and Ayisha seem to imply that almost anything is possible if you can make your dream—and then act on it.

"We Were Like a Little Construction Crew." When the children talk about the three-dimensional structures they build and then play in, they often portray themselves as co-workers and co-thinkers. For example, Michael explains: "So me and Allen thought of something: 'What can we do?' Then we looked at the pillows and the blanket and we went like [said], 'Ahhh, maybe we could do this.'" Working together "like a little construction crew," children actively and purposefully shape, order, and give meaning to the world around them.

To Hide and Find Sanctuary. Building places by and for themselves matters to the children in this study. They use these private, sometimes secret places as hideouts and sanctuaries. Inside, they feel safe and protected because, as Rex says, they are "isolated from the rest of the world."

Children's constructions, even though fragile and temporary, provide them with opportunities to re-create the world for and by themselves. These special places are stages or platforms where children act like and act on what matters to them, making a home for themselves in the world.

To Pretend Is to Learn. This study reveals that children actively learn about others and a wider world by assuming roles, tasks, and taking another's perspective. Michelle explains that by pretending to be a bank teller and a mother, she prepares for the future—she "knows how it feels" and she will know "things about . . . being a person that works at a bank or being a person who has to run around and find a baby-sitter." Rex lives in the city and likes to play basketball but can nonetheless imagine himself "like an Eskimo" girl whose story he read in school. The enclosure he builds may differ in location and materials, yet the underlying significance seems in many ways similar. Brenda sets up a tent in her bedroom and calls it "REALly camping." It works, she explains, because you pretend you are someplace else. Luigi Pirandello (1915/1990), the author of many dramas, provides this clue to children's ability to take their play seriously: "The wonder is in themselves; they impart it to the things with which they are playing, and let themselves be deceived by them. It is no longer a game; it is a wonderful reality" (p. 87).

"Fun" Is Serious, Complex, and Purposeful. This study reveals that as they build and play, children make sure they are having fun. That fun is a basic criterion for what children do on their own may seem an "obvious" point. However, in the examples that follow, we can see something of its complexity and significance.

Michelle uses the word *fun* to describe one reason for pretending to be a mother even though she's still a child. By doing so, she says she learns how it feels to be a responsible, caring adult. Brenda explains that *fun* is feeling like you are camping out in the woods in a teepee. She and her cousin, however, are really in Brenda's bedroom, under a pink satin bedcover held up by two carefully slanted chairs. On their own, the girls create the context and ambiance they want—what Brenda calls "really spooky and everything." She explains, "And we go to the library to get the books—spooky books—so we could read [them inside the teepee]." In these ways the girls take charge of a particular space to create a special place for themselves where experience, story, and imagination mingle— a world they make just scary enough to be fun.

Michael elaborates on what having fun means for him when he plays cops and robbers with his younger brother inside the family's apartment. He says the game is *fun* because he has permission as a robber "to be sneaky" and because he can send his younger brother off to jail (it's written into the script). But what makes cops and robbers the most fun, Michael adds, are the times when both parents are away at work (that's when the boys can play freely throughout the entire apartment).

When children talk of what they do and play on their own, they use the word *fun* as shorthand to describe complex actions and strong feelings. It seems they are following their own purposes and engaged in what matters to them, including feelings of control and mastery.

Children Dream New Worlds. This study confirms children's capacities to imagine new worlds, to care enough to build them, and to believe that they can. Pointing to her drawing of the clubhouse she and friends built in a crabapple tree, Ayisha talks about "managing her dream":

> AYISHA: It was fine; it was perfect. We got to look out/out and see how it looks. And how it feel to be in there and everything (*her voice is very soft*).
> SALLY: How does it feel?
> AYISHA: It feels like you're in a/a house 'cause it's fresh. Sometimes it's fresh up in the tree, you wouldn't smell nothing. It smells cle-an and stuff, clean and stuff.
> SALLY: What do you mean when you use that phrase, "managing your dream"?
> AYISHA: That I got to do it, and my dream has come true, and I had/I BELIEVED in it. That's what I mean by managing it.

LESSONS FOR EDUCATORS

By making visible how, through their play, children give form and identity to themselves, I hope to help classroom teachers connect children's lives in school with the richness and vitality of the worlds children create for themselves outside of school. The deficit model asserts that poor city kids are "troubled," "passive," and "dumb." Sadly, that model persistently permeates our society and often underlies discussions of educational reform. This study challenges these assertions and labels them misconceptions. My analysis of children's strengths, when informed by the experience and thinking of educators, leads to three suggestions for supporting "smart" kids in urban schools. Briefly, they are for teachers to (1) create a rich environment, (2) allow children to participate actively in their learning, and (3) teach by listening.

Create a Rich Environment

This study reveals how children take advantage of local environments to create places for their play (e.g., small bedrooms, a crowded playground, and a tree that can be climbed). It also uncovers how, in children's hands and imaginations, "things" are shaped into three-dimensional structures, made into tools, and become something else (e.g., three pillows and a bedcover become a bakery; rock, string, and stick make a hammer; a statue of a seal is transformed into a car).

The work of two experienced and observant teacher/researchers, Susan Isaacs and Frances Hawkins, informs this point. Their writings are "dated" in that they describe work 70 and 30 years ago, respectively; nevertheless, their thinking and their work provide rich, practical information for us today relating to the "things" and "surroundings" that support children's active interest in learning. I will take some time to talk about these two remarkable teacher/researchers as they help set the context for the suggestions that follow.

Susan Isaacs (1968), founder of a small private school in England in the 1920s, argues that the "environment itself" is the main stimulus for children's activity. She writes: "We aimed at arranging the physical surroundings in the schoolroom or garden so as to provoke the children to active and constructive pursuits" (p. 33). Some of the materials, tools, and spaces made available to Isaacs's students were clay, chalk, plasticine, paint, Bunsen burners, lumber, hammers, saws, hoses and tubes, buckets, cloth and needles and thread, beads, thermometers, pots and pans, "dress-up" clothes, records and record player, sand pile, vegetable and flower garden, shovels, ladder, rabbits, and dissecting tools (one of the rabbits died and the children dissected it, their interest lasting many days). Additionally, with easy access to yard and garden, and encouraged by their teachers, children brought bones, earthworms, a spider, and caterpillars inside for closer observation.

In *The Logic of Action*, Frances Hawkins (1974), noted teacher of young children and teacher of teachers, describes her weekly visits in 1969 to a class of 4-year-old deaf children in an urban public school in the United States. In the final pages of her account, Hawkins provides an inventory of the things she's brought in over the semester for the children to explore. The list includes apparatus for making soap bubbles, flashlights, a hamster, balances, clear plastic containers, a prism, funnels, eye droppers, food coloring, alarm clocks (to take apart), colored gels, pulleys, plastic tubing, a screwdriver and screws, and nuts and bolts (other items she mentions as wanting to bring—hammers, nails, and wood, for example—were not permitted by the school authorities).

Teachers today, as Isaacs and Hawkins before them, can thoughtfully create classroom environments where an abundance of things are within children's reach. Books, posters, and computers, however, are not enough; it takes a variety of supplies, materials, tools, equipment, and real things (such as flowers and spiders) to invite children's curiosity, promote their explorations, and allow them to make things, build things, and make sense of things.

Allow Children to Participate Actively

In general, adults control the physical environments where children live, play, and attend school. At school, for instance, adults make all or most of the important decisions about time, space, and things; and outdoors, adults (albeit only a few) decide what is built where—a parking lot instead of a playground, for example. Adults also make all the important decisions about learning.

That teachers may stand in children's way even when the environment they provide is safe and well endowed reminds me of my conversation with a fifth grader. We were talking about what science activities he did in school when he asked: "How come Einstein and Edison got to invent everything and we don't?" Thinking about my extended observations in his classroom, I saw his point. He was fortunate in that the suburban school he attended was clean and safe; his classroom was uncrowded and airy and students often worked in small groups. Their work, however, was all the same, often with paper and pencil, and almost every question the children worked on was posed by their teacher.

It is difficult for children to be inventive in teacher-centered classrooms. Sociologist Dan Lortie's (1975) haunting image of a teacher standing alone on a stage is, he argues, the prevailing model. Such need not be the case if teachers make room for a supporting cast—one that is enthusiastic, energetic, talented, and just waiting to be called in from the wings. This alternative scenario puts children front and center with real opportunities to make the scenery, adjust the lighting, and arrange the set—in other words, to co-construct an environment for learning and doing.

The children in this study remind us that we can enliven classrooms through opportunities for dramatic play. The teepee Brenda's second-grade teacher made with paper and sticks comes to mind. For Brenda, the effect was consequential—it was the impetus for her becoming an expert teepee-builder and storyteller. She did this work in her bedroom, continually making her play fresh by varying light and sound and by infusing the narrative with ideas selected from books and movies. And although play such as Brenda's may necessarily work better at home than at school, the stories that children perform at home and on the playground can be viewed as fodder for their activities in the classroom.

Variations on "circle time" as developed by teachers of young children (see, e.g., Jones & Nimmo, 1994; Paley, 1981) are helpful examples of ways to acknowledge children's inner lives and facilitate what "children already know but don't yet know they know" (Wagner, 1976, p. 13).

As for older children, thanks to biographer Betty Jane Wagner (1976), we have a detailed account and analysis of the work of Dorothy Heathcote, who taught drama to school children, youth, and adults, mainly in England, in the 1960s and 1970s. For Heathcote, dramatic play allows children to develop the capacity to identify with the "other" and thus gain new insight about and for themselves. Moreover, drama, as she puts it, is a way to help "children find that they, too, have something in common with all that has gone before. They, too, belong to humanity" (p. 19). Children learn, for example, that some dreams—their own included—have been dreamed by others.

Teach by Listening

Eleanor Duckworth (1987/1996) writes about the importance of teachers working with one student to "learn more about learning" (p. 62). "As teachers," Duckworth urges, "we need to respect the meaning our students are giving to the events that we share. In the interest of making connections between their understanding and ours, we must adopt an insider's view: seek to understand their sense as well as help them understand ours" (p. 112).

For an example, I return to Isaac's mother, who told me she became more aware of the value in her son's play when she, in the role of photographer, documented it. Previously she had paid little attention to what he was doing and was content that he was safe and being entertained: "Oh, good, he's doing something/something to just, you know, keep himself busy. That's fine." She continues:

> I never thought his playing as something that he was learning or
> that he was really entertaining himself. I never saw how serious he
> can be about his play and how imaginative he can be about his
> characters. . . . I mean, you figure, they're sitting in front of
> Nintendo, they're playing Nintendo—that's great. But when he does
> things like this—like inventing stories with dinosaurs—and I hear
> his vocabulary, and I say, YEA (*she claps*).

In the above quotation, Isaac's mother points out her son's rich vocabulary, the inventive quality of his stories, his ease in remembering the names of his toys, the seriousness he brings to his play, his creative use of space and materials, and his engrossment. She calls what he does a combination of "learning" and "entertainment" and contrasts its value to his "sitting in front" of a video game. Whether parent or teacher, by "listening in" and observing children when they play on their own, we may notice and value how smart kids really are.

ADULTS AS WORLDMAKERS

What would our schools and neighborhoods look like "if we put our minds to it"? This phrase, quoted earlier, is Ayisha's. She also provides us with a verb—"imaginate"—employing it when she refers to her actions to construct that world. Although Ayisha's own dream house is elaborately designed, above yet connected to both home and community, the world she wishes for is neither fantastical nor extravagant. It is a place that feels clean and fresh; a quiet place; located with grocery store and kitchen close by; one that her friends will visit; and where she will have access to a TV, VCR, and radio.

As adults, we are left with two important tasks. We must "imaginate" worlds where children are safe and never go hungry; where their thoughts, dreams, work, and play are acknowledged and valued; where there is an abundance of "loose parts" (Nicholson, 1971), a bag of tools for making and fixing things, and a choice of spaces, some for digging, climbing, running, some for sitting quietly. Moreover, such places must be within skipping distance. And we must form construction crews to build these worlds—not just for a few children as we do now, but for all children. Signs saying "Under Construction" must be everywhere.

APPENDIX
Details of the Study

SCHOOL AND DISTRICT DEMOGRAPHICS

According to information provided by School District 4 Office in 1995, the district serves approximately 14,000 students in pre-kindergarten through the ninth grade. The student population is 61% Hispanic, 36% black, and 3% white and other. Eighty-eight percent of the students receive a free lunch and 41% are eligible for Chapter I services. New immigrant students account for 6% of the total student population.

The East Harlem community is a low-income, minority neighborhood with an ethnic mix of Hispanic (42%), black (44%), white (11%), and other (3%) cultures. It is a community characterized by poverty and social problems. The median family income of $14,884 is one of the lowest in New York City. Forty percent of all families receive public assistance. Households headed by single parents (54.2%) predominate. The community has the highest infant mortality rate in New York City; 14% of live births are to low-birth-weight children. East Harlem has the highest incidence of AIDS in the city and 28% of the total pediatric AIDS cases in the entire United States.

The school, designated a Chapter I school, serves approximately 700 children in pre-kindergarten through sixth grade and has an average daily attendance of 88.2%. The student body is 56% Hispanic, 35% black, and 9% Native American, Asian, and white. Thirty percent of the students read at or above grade level, below the district average of 36%.

INTERVIEW SCHEDULE

I begin the interview by introducing myself and learning the child's name (later on in the interview I ask for age and address and how long the child has lived at that address and attended the school).

I say I am interested in what children do and play on their own. As I did in the pilot study, I add that I am "doing research," I ask the children what that means for them and thus have an opportunity to clarify my activities should that be necessary.

I say that what they say to me is not for a "grade" and I will not repeat it to anyone. I say that if they don't want to answer a question, they don't have to; moreover, we can stop at any time.

I next ask each child to use the large paper and pencils I have provided to make a drawing of the places where he or she plays. I wait to see if there is need for clarification; for example, a child might ask, "Inside my apartment?" or "By myself?" I accept whatever direction the child suggests.

After children have drawn, I ask each child to tell me about his or her drawing, beginning

> **Take me on a tour. Tell me what you do and what happens here.**
>   or
> **Please take me on a tour of your neighborhood (your apartment) and tell me about the places you have drawn and what you do there. I won't say too much—I want you to talk.**

I might use these prompts:

> **What do you like to play most?**
> **Where do you like to play the most?**
>
> **Let me make sure I've got straight most of everything you say you play indoors (outdoors); there's ____ and ____, etc. Are there any others?**
>
> **Now I'd like to ask you to say some more about ____.**
> **Now I'd like to ask you to tell me something about what you do outdoors/indoors.**

About outdoor play, I ask:

> **What's your favorite time of year to play outdoors?**
> **Tell me about what you do then.**
> **How do you get there?**
> **How is that different from playing in the winter? summer?**

About indoor play, I ask:

> **Do you like to play inside? (If yes) Tell me about what you play.**

About both inside and outside play, I ask:

> **Do you play mostly by yourself or with others?**
>
> **What kinds of things do you do alone/with others?**

Do you play mostly with boys? girls?
Do you play mostly with brothers? sisters? kids from school? kids
   from your building or on your block? cousins?

Ever build anything? Make anything?
(If "Yes") Tell me about it.
      or
Some people say kids build things. What's been your experience?

Ever build anything you could get into?
(If "Yes") Tell me about how it got going.
How did the idea come about?
Tell me about who was involved.
Who was there?
Tell me about how you went about doing this.
What else did you have to do?
What did you use? (materials and tools)
Where did you get them?
How did the work go?
Any problems? What happened?
What were the hard parts? the easy?

Tell me some more about what you did with what you built.

What again do you call it?

Tell me again who plays there.
What are their ages?
How did you get to know these kids?

What is it like inside?
Did you have anything inside? What? Where did you get them?
Why did you bring _____ inside?

Tell me about what happened to your (name of structure).

Have you made things like this before?
Do you know other kids who have made things like this?

Any rules or something like that?
Like, who can play there and who can't?
Who decides?

How do you know someone "belongs"/can come in?
Is what you do "make-believe" or "for real"? How do you see it?

What advice do you have for other kids who want to make a
_____ and don't know what to do?
How might they start?
Where might be best to build?
Where to get stuff to do it?

Is being there like being at school (home)? Why? Why not?

What's the nicest thing about your (*name of structure*)?
How often do you go there?

If I was passing by, would I have seen you?
If I could see you, what would I see you doing?
What might other people think you were doing?

Did you tell anybody about what you made? were doing?

Suppose I was a new kid in your building/on your block and I
    didn't know much about where to play around here. What
    would you tell me?

Suppose I was a kid (try same gender/try opposite) and wanted to
    join you. Tell me how that might happen.

What else do you play?
Ever play house, store, restaurant—something like that?
Where?
What do you do?
What do you call it?
Are you playing by yourself? with others? (If others) Tell me about
    who they are and what they like to play.
Whose idea was it and how did it get started?
Do you play with dolls? Lego-men?
Do any cooking?
What else do you do?
What other things do you use when you play this?
Do you think of what you do as make-believe, or is it "for real," or
    sometimes, is it both?

CONTACT SUMMARY

Child's #: Age: _____   Birth date: _____   Grade: _____
Address: _____   Street coordinates: ____
Years lived there _____   Where else lived and how long? _____
_____
People in same household, relationship and ages: _____
_____

Years attended   How does child get to school?
this school _____   Walk/public bus/subway/school bus
Interview # _____   Date: _____ Time: ____ to ____

Place interview takes place: _____

1. Child's appearance: _____
2. Child's demeanor and responsiveness to situation and to specifics of
   the interview: _____
3. Child's approaches to drawing: _____
4. Child's approach to photographs: _____
5. Synopsis of contact: _____
6. Main issues or themes that seemed to emerge: _____
7. Key words and phrases used once or repeated by child: _____
8. Places child says plays (circle):
   inside apartment: bedroom bathroom kitchen living room
   inside apartment building: hallway stairs basement
   outside: schoolyard park playground sidewalk vacant lot
        abandoned building   around buildings   (other): _____
9. How child plays: alone
                     with others: siblings cousins friends
                                   younger older
                                   same sex mixed
                     size of groupings: _____
10. Other points that seemed salient, interesting, illuminating or
    important in this contact: _____
11. Impressions, hypotheses, hints related to research questions: _____
12. Any concerns child seems to have or I have: _____
13. What I should follow-up or seek in next contact? _____
14. What should I bring? _____

DRAWING SUMMARY FORM

Child's number: _____ Age: _____ Interview date: _____

Version of drawing: # ___

Names of "Readers" [those people looking at the drawing with me]: _____
_____ _____

Today's date: _____

1. A sketch of child's drawing: _____

2. What are the materials used? _____

3. What do I (we) see? (lines, angles, shapes, symmetry, overlaps): _____
_____

4. What does the drawing seem to represent? (design, story, scene, symbol): _____

5. How is it organized? (perspective, composition, action, view, completion): _____

6. What kinds of feelings seem to be here? (humor, persuasion, information, etc.): _____

7. Where might the idea(s) come from? (imagination, observation, literature, TV, imitation, conversation, interview itself):_____

8. List additions, if any, from earlier versions: _____

9. List changes, if any, from earlier versions: _____

10. What words and phrases did child use in describing picture that want to note? _____

11. What do I want to follow-up and pick up on in next session? _____
_____

12. Attach reduced photocopy of child's drawing.

Source: Adapted from Engel, 1991

References

Acher, R. A. (1904). Spontaneous constructions and primitive activities of children analogous to those of primitive man. *American Journal of Psychology, 21,* 114–150.

Barker, R. G., & Wright, H. F. (1966). *One boy's day: A specimen record of behavior.* Hamden, CT: Archon Books. (Original work published 1951)

Bauman, R. (1982). Ethnography of children's folklore. In P. Gilmore & A. A. Glatthorn (Eds.), *Children in and out of school: Ethnography and education* (pp. 172–186). Washington, DC: Center for Applied Linguistics.

Becker, F. D. (1976). Children's play in multifamily housing. *Environment and Behavior, 8*(4), 545–574.

Berg, M., & Medrich, E. A. (1980). Children in four neighborhoods: The physical environment and its effect on play and play patterns. *Environment and Behavior, 12*(3), 320–348.

Block, J. H. (1976). Debatable conclusions about sex differences. *Contemporary Psychology, 21*(8), 517–522.

Boyer, P. (1978). *Urban masses and moral order in America, 1820–1920.* Cambridge, MA: Harvard University Press.

Brace, C. L. (1872). *The dangerous classes of New York and twenty years' work among them.* New York: Wynkoop & Hallenbeck.

Cooper, C. C. (1970, October). Adventure playgrounds. *Landscape Architecture,* pp. 18–23.

Cooper, M. (1990). Selected photographs. In A. Dargan & S. Zeitlin (Eds.), *City play.* New Brunswick, NJ: Rutgers University Press.

Cooper Marcus, C., & Moore, R. C. (1976). Children and their environments: A review of research. *Journal of Architectural Education, 24*(4), 22–25.

Covello, L. (1970). *The heart is the teacher: The teacher in the urban community.* Totowa, NJ: Littlefield, Adams & Co. (Original work published 1958)

Culin, S. (1891). Street games in Brooklyn, N. Y. *Journal of American Folk-lore,* 4, 221–237.

Dewey, J. (1980). *Art as experience.* New York: Perigee. (Original work published 1934)

Duckworth, E. (1996). *"The having of wonderful ideas" and other essays on teaching and learning* (2nd ed.). New York: Teachers College Press. (Original work published 1987)

Engel, B. S. (1991). *Looking and summarizing qualitative data*. Unpublished manuscript, Lesley College, Cambridge, MA.

Fine, G. A., & Sandstrom, K. L. (1988). *Knowing children: Participant observation with minors*. Newbury Park, CA: Sage.

Finnan, C. R. (1988). The ethnography of children's spontaneous play. In G. Spindler (Ed.), *Doing the ethnography of schooling: Educational anthropology in action* (pp. 356–380). Prospect Heights, IL: Waveland Press.

Franklin, M. B. (1983). Play as the creation of imaginary situations: The role of language. In S. Wapner & B. Kaplan (Eds.), *Toward a holistic developmental psychology*. Hillsdale, NJ: Erlbaum.

Garabino, J., Stott, F. M., & Faculty of the Erikson Institute. (1989). *What children can tell us: Eliciting, interpreting, and evaluating information from children*. San Francisco: Jossey-Bass.

Glassner, B. (1976). Kid society. *Urban Education, 11*(1), 5–22.

Goodman, N. (1978). *Ways of worldmaking*. Indianapolis: Hackett.

Hall, G. S. (1975). Boy life in a Massachusetts country town forty years ago (pp. 300–322). In T. L. Smith (Ed.), *Aspects of child life and education*. New York: Arno. (Original work published 1907)

Hart, R. (1979). *Children's experience of place*. New York: Irvington.

Hawes, J. M., & Hiner, N. R. (Eds.). (1985). *American childhood: A research guide and historical handbook*. London: Greenwood Press.

Hawkins, F. P. (1974). *The logic of action*. New York: Pantheon Books.

Howard, A., & Scott, R. A. (1981). The study of minority groups in complex societies. In R. H. Munroe, R. L. Munroe, & B. B. Whiting (Eds.), *Handbook of cross-cultural human development* (pp. 113–152). New York: Garland STPM Press.

Isaacs, S. (1968). *Intellectual growth in young children*. New York: Schocken Books.

Jacobs, J. (1961). *The death and life of great American cities*. New York: Vintage Books.

James, W. (1983). *The principles of psychology*. Cambridge, MA: Harvard University Press. (Original work published 1890)

Jones, E., & Nimmo, J. (1994). *Emergent curriculum*. Washington, DC: National Association for the Education of Young Children.

Ladd, F. (1970). Black youths view their environment: Neighborhood maps. *Environment and Behavior, 2*(1), 74–99.

Ladd, F. (1972). Black youths view their environments: Some views of housing. *Journal of the American Institute of Planners, 38*(2), 108–116.

Lerner, P. (1959). *My own yard to play in* [Film]. New York: McGraw-Hill.

Lever, J. (1976). Sex differences in the games children play. *Social Problems, 23*, 478–487.

Levitt, H. (1987). *In the street*. Durham, NC: Duke University Press.

Levitt, H. (1989). *A way of seeing*. Durham, NC: Duke University Press.

Lortie, D. C. (1975). *Schoolteacher: A sociological study*. Chicago: University of Chicago Press.

Maccoby, E. E. (1990). Gender and relationships: A developmental account. *American Psychologist, 45*(4), 513–520.

Mauer, R., & Baxter, J. C. (1972). Images of the neighborhood and city among Black, Anglo-, and Mexican American children. *Environment and Behavior, 4*(4), 351–388.

Mechling, J. (1980). Sacred and profane play in the Boy Scouts of America. In H. B. Swartzman (Ed.), *Play and culture* (pp. 206–215). West Point, NY: Leisure Press.

Michelson, W., Levine, S. V., & Spina, A.-R. (1979). *The child in the city.* Toronto: University of Toronto Press.

Moore, R. C. (1980). Collaborating with young people to assess their landscape values. *Ekistics, 47*(281), 128–135.

Moore, W. (1969). *The vertical ghetto: Everyday life in an urban project.* New York: Random House.

Newson, J., & Newson, E. (1979). *Toys and playthings in development and remediation.* New York: Pantheon Books.

Nicholson, S. (1971). How not to cheat children: The theory of loose parts. *Landscape Architecture, 63*(1), 30–34.

Olsen, T. (1974). *Yonnondio.* New York: Dell.

Opie, I., & Opie, P. (1984). *Children's games in street and playground.* New York: Oxford University Press. (Original work published 1969)

Paley, V. G. (1981). *Wally's stories: Conversations in kindergarten.* Cambridge, MA: Harvard University Press.

Pirandello, L. (1990). *The notebooks of Serafino of Gubbio.* Sawtoy, UK: Dedalus. (Original work published 1915)

Riis, J. A. (1971). *How the other half lives.* New York: Dover. (Original work published 1890)

Rogoff, B. (1990). *Apprenticeship in thinking: Cognitive development in social context.* New York: Oxford University Press.

Selltiz, C., Wrightsman, L. S., & Cook, S. W. (1976). *Research methods in social relations.* New York: Holt, Rinehart & Winston.

Sluckin, A. (1981). *Growing up in the playground: The social development of children.* London: Routledge & Kegan Paul.

Sobel, D. (1993). *Children's special places: Exploring the role of forts, dens, and bush houses in middle childhood.* Tucson, AZ: Zephyr Press.

Sutton-Smith, B. (1982). Play theory of the rich and for the poor. In P. Gilmore & A. A. Glatthorn (Eds.), *Children in and out of school* (pp. 187–202). Washington: Ethnography and Education Center for Applied Linguistics.

Thorne, B. (1993). *Gender play: Girl and boys in school.* New Brunswick, NJ: Rutgers University Press.

Wagner, B. J. (1976). *Dorothy Heathcote: Drama as a learning medium.* Washington, DC: National Education Association.

White, S. H., & Siegel, A. W. (1984). Cognitive development in time and space. In B. Rogoff & J. Lave (Eds.), *Everyday cognition: It's development in social context* (pp. 238–277) Cambridge, MA: Harvard University Press.

Whiting, B. B., & Edwards, C. P. (1988). *Children of different worlds: The formation of social behavior.* Cambridge, MA: Harvard University Press.

Winnicott, D. W. (1983). *Home is where we start from: Essays by a psychoanalyst.* New York: Norton.

Wohlwill, J. F., & Heft, H. (1987). The physical environment and the development of the child. In D. Stokols & I. Altman (Eds.), *Handbook of environmental psychology* (pp. 281–321). New York: Wiley.

Wright, H. F. (1960). Observational child study. In P. H. Mussen (Ed.), *Handbook of research methods in child development* (pp. 71–133). New York: Wiley.

Zerner, C. (1977, Autumn). The street hearth of play: Children in the city. *Landscape, 22*(1), 19–30.

Index

About the Author

SALLY MIDDLEBROOKS is director of education for the Association of Science-Technology Centers, Incorporated, in Washington, D.C. She earned an M.S.Ed. in early childhood education from Bank Street College of Education, an M.S. in environmental studies from Antioch/New England Graduate School, and an Ed.D. from the Harvard Graduate School of Education. She directed a natural science program called the Nature Shop for the Boys' Club of New York and managed Belvedere Castle, the Central Park Learning Center. As director of education for the Central Park Conservancy, she co-authored with Mr. Bick's sixth-grade class at P.S. 146 the pamphlet *Mu-se'-um: The story of how one teacher and his class constructed a museum from their explorations of Central Park* (1991).